H. C. Trumbull

Hints on Bible Study

H. C. Trumbull
Hints on Bible Study
ISBN/EAN: 9783337172893

Printed in Europe, USA, Canada, Australia, Japan

Cover: Foto ©Lupo / pixelio.de

More available books at **www.hansebooks.com**

HINTS ON BIBLE STUDY

Copyright, 1897,
BY
JOHN D. WATTLES & CO.

PREFACE

Never before since the earlier books of the Bible were written, was the Bible as a book so much in use, or so highly valued by men of the highest scholarship as well as by the common people the world over—in Christian lands and beyond. Never before were so many interested in Bible study, or so desirous of having a part in such study.

Yet it is unmistakably true that very many who have a real interest in the Bible, and who want to gain practical help from it, have but vague ideas as to just what Bible study is, and as to the right spirit in which it should be prosecuted. Still more are in ignorance as to the best methods of studying the Bible in its different portions, and for its varied important uses.

It is in view of the widespread interest in Bible study, and of the wider spread need of information and help on the subject, that this little volume of Hints has been compiled for the benefit of all who share this interest and this need. They are at the best but hints; yet for that very reason they may be more helpful than an exhaustive treatise would prove.

The chapters have been culled largely from the pages of The Sunday School Times, of recent years and earlier; yet several of them were written within the past few months expressly for this volume. A peculiar interest attaches to the articles by the late Drs. Austin Phelps and John A. Broadus, on subjects of perennial interest; and to those by Bishop C. J. Ellicott and Dr. J. L. M. Curry, written some time ago, yet as fresh and timely now as when first written.

It will be seen, however, that these Hints

are arranged according to a well-defined plan; and it is hoped that the compiler, who has gathered these things from those pages, will be deemed "like unto a man that is a householder, which bringeth forth out of his treasure things new and old" for the supply and nourishment of the children of the kingdom.

CONTENTS

	Page
WHAT IS BIBLE STUDY?	1
By H. Clay Trumbull, D.D.	
RIGHT SPIRIT IN BIBLE STUDY	15
By Professor Austin Phelps, D.D.	
INDUCTIVE AND DEDUCTIVE METHODS OF STUDY	35
By President Robert Ellis Thompson, S.T.D.	
STUDYING THE BIBLE BOOK BY BOOK .	49
By Professor F. K. Sanders, Ph.D.	
SCRIPTURE EXPLAINING SCRIPTURE . .	67
By Professor J. L. M. Curry, D.D., LL.D.	
STUDY OF THE BIBLE AS LITERATURE . .	79
By Professor George B. Stevens, Ph.D., D.D.	
HINTS AS TO BIBLE INTERPRETATION . .	97
By President John A. Broadus, D.D., LL.D.	
NEED OF ORIENTAL LIGHTS ON THE BIBLE	109
By H. Clay Trumbull, D.D.	

CONTENTS

	Page
GLEANINGS FROM THE BIBLE MARGINS	121

By Professor John H. Bernard, D.D.

PLACE OF HELPS IN BIBLE STUDY . . . 141
By H. Clay Trumbull, D.D.

HOW TO USE BIBLE COMMENTARIES . . 155
By the Right Rev. C. J. Ellicott, D.D.
Bishop of Gloucester and Bristol

RIGHT SPIRIT IN OLD TESTAMENT STUDY 173
By Professor Willis J. Beecher, D.D.

HOW TO GET A KNOWLEDGE OF THE WHOLE
NEW TESTAMENT 191
By Professor George B. Stevens, Ph.D., D.D.

HINTS ON THE STUDY OF THE GOSPELS . 205
By Professor M. B. Riddle, D.D., LL.D.

HINTS ON THE STUDY OF THE EPISTLES . 217
By Professor J. M. Stifler, D.D.

THE BIBLE AS A GUIDE IN SOCIAL STUDIES 235
By President Robert Ellis Thompson, S.T.D.

UNATTAINED IDEAL OF BIBLE STUDY . . 245
By Bishop John H. Vincent, D.D., LL.D.

WHAT IS BIBLE STUDY?

WHAT IS BIBLE STUDY?

BY H. CLAY TRUMBULL, D.D.

A great deal is said, in these days, of the importance and value of Bible study. On the one hand, there are those who enjoin it as a duty and a privilege; and, on the other hand, there are those who tell of its pleasure and gain to themselves. Yet it is by no means clear that those who press the duty of Bible study have in mind the same kind of studying as that which is found precious and profitable by those who tell of their experience in this line; and the question is still an open one, What is Bible study? What is that study of the Bible in which all Christians ought to have a part, and which is sure to be beneficial to those who give themselves to it?

It is not enough to say that "we should study the Bible as we study any other book;" for, in the first place, the Bible is very different from other books, and, in the second place, we do not study books, other than the Bible, in precisely the same way. The study of dictionaries is one thing, the study of mathematical works is another thing. That which would be wise study of a book on chemistry would not meet the case in a volume of history, or biography, or poetry. The Bible includes history, biography, poetry, ethics, theology, and a great many other themes; how can the Bible be studied so as to give one a mastery of its structure and contents on the one hand, and of its teachings and practical applications on the other? What is wise Bible study, and how is it to be undertaken?

Bible reading may be an important element in Bible study, but the reading of the Bible is not in itself the study of the Bible.

There are those who have read the Bible through in course, over and over again, year after year, without ever giving five minutes of their lives to honest and intelligent Bible study. They have perhaps felt that there was a certain merit in the reading of a stated portion of the Bible every morning and evening, as others have felt that there was a merit in the "saying" of their prayers; but they have not read the Bible as a means of Bible study. Old Thomas Fuller has this sort of conventional Bible reading in mind, when he says: "Lord, I discover an arrant laziness in my soul. For when I am to read a chapter in the Bible, before I begin it I look where it endeth. And if it endeth not on the same side I cannot keep my hands from turning over the leaf to measure the length thereof on the other side; if it swells to many verses, I begin to grudge. Surely my heart is not rightly affected." And this frank confession is that which many a Bible reader could attest as his own, because Bible reading is by no means Bible studying. If a traveler in a strange country were seeking information as to his course from a standard guide-book, he would not complain of the fulness of detail there given as he studied its pages. And if a poor man had found a book telling how any person could become rich, he would hardly be likely to begrudge an added page of counsel in the direction of his life pursuit. But here is a difference between merely reading a book, and studying it with a purpose!

Bible memorizing has its incidental advantages to one who would have the words of Scripture always available; but Bible memorizing is never in itself Bible studying, nor is it even, like Bible reading, an important element in Bible study. It is an aid to the using of the Bible, rather than to its studying. There is at least one well-authenticated case of an ordinarily intelligent man who had memorized the entire Bible, so that he could repeat its every verse with fluency, yet who was not only ignorant of the way of salvation, but was unacquainted with both the lesser and the greater teachings of the Bible. Bible memorizing may be made a real help to the student of the Bible, and again it may stand in the way of Bible knowledge through its permanently fixing a wrong idea in the mind; but, in any event, Bible memorizing should never be confounded with Bible studying.

Familiarizing one's self with the contents of the Bible, so as to be able, off-hand, to locate the book and chapter and verse of any historic fact or special teaching, requires a certain measure of application in study; but it can hardly be called in itself Bible study, any more than Bible memorizing can be. Neither intellectual nor spiritual power is requisite for this sort of memory filling; and he who is a master in such surface acquaintance with the contents of the Bible may be without any true knowledge of Bible teachings, or any practical results of true Bible study. Alexander Cruden, who located every principal word and phrase in the entire Bible, seems hardly to have been a Bible student, in the sense of becoming familiar with the sense and spirit of Bible teachings; and he was rightly looked upon as mildly and inoffensively lunatic,—whether, as some thought, because of the bite of a mad dog, or, as others supposed, because of his disappointment in love, it matters little. There was certainly no enlargement of his mind or soul by the special work on the Bible to which he gave himself. There are obvious advantages in a close familiarity with the verbal contents of the Bible; but the securing of this kind of knowledge must not be identified with the wise study of the Bible.

A careful analysis of the various books of the Bible, with a view to showing their date and authorship and immediate purpose of writing, together with an exhibit of their peculiarities of style and subject-matter, calls for patient investigation, and demands a large measure of intellectual acumen; but all this knowledge may be mastered without touching the great truths of those books severally, which have a perennial value, and which are of chiefest importance to him who would know and use the Bible aright. It were possible for a student of the Old Testament books to learn everything about those books, without learning or seeking to learn from the books themselves those profound spiritual teachings which distinguish them from all other sacred writings of their time. It were possible for a student of the four Gospels to master all the distinctive peculiarities of each one of them separately for a comparison with the other three, without really gaining more of personal help in his spiritual life than if he had been studying the Rig Vedas or the suras of the Qurân. Such study is well enough in its way, for those who have time and taste and ability for it; but it ought not to stand in the place of that study of the Bible which will enable one to learn what the Bible alone can impart to a student.

Tracking the use of a particular word or phrase throughout the Bible record, in proof of a pre-supposed duty or doctrine, without discriminating between the different meanings of that word or phrase in different connections, may be a means of Bible study that is not Bible study. Its results are liable to be misleading or confusing, through a lack of that study of the Bible which seeks to gain instruction and inspiration from its pages, instead of looking there only for proof-texts in support of preconceived opinions. No one Bible text is to be taken merely by itself as covering all that the Bible teaches concerning the main theme of that text, nor is the apparent teaching of that text to be made the means of interpreting every other text which has a verbal similarity thereto. Text-collating is not by any means the true study of texts.

Bible study may include any or all of these methods of Bible examination; but it must include something beyond them all in order to be true Bible study. There is a sense in which the Bible is like any other book, in being made up of words that must be noted in their connection and uses, and that therefore it is to be studied like any other book in order to arrive at its meanings. But there is another sense in which the Bible is unlike all other books, in that it contains God's peculiar message to mankind through men whom he trained and inspired for that special purpose, and that therefore its study must be mainly for the ascertaining and understanding of the divine truths that, unlike any other book, it has for ourselves as we are in our present needs and our ultimate destiny. Except for this difference in methods and objects of study, the Bible study of the baldest rationalist and of the most frigid agnostic is as much of a help toward truth as the Bible study of the warmest-hearted and most trustful Christian believer.

He who would study the Bible must bear in mind that it is not the books of the Bible that were themselves inspired, but that it was the writers of these books whom God inspired for their writing. "Men spake from God, being moved by the Holy Ghost." One man wrote at one time and in one style, and another man wrote at another time and in another style. One wrote in poetic imagery, and another in didactic prose. A perception of these differences is essential to an understanding of the truths thus declared from God. But the main purpose of this sacred record of inspired teachings—whoever was the writer, and whensoever and howsoever he wrote—is the instruction and guidance and inspiration of their believing student. "Every scripture inspired of God is . . . profitable for teaching, for reproof, for correction, for instruction which is in righteousness: that the man of God may be complete, furnished completely unto every good work." Hence no Bible study looks to the proper end of Bible study that does not seek to ascertain just what lesson it is that God would have this student gain from the passage immediately under study;

and no student of the Bible has yet profited by his Bible study unless he is thereby helped toward truer completeness of manhood as a disciple of Christ.

It is well enough to become closely familiar with the structure and contents of the different books of the Bible, and to memorize as many portions of it as there is time and mental strength for; but all this is but an incident to true Bible study, and not the thing itself. Bible study is for the purpose of gaining impulses and helps to the Christian life. In view of this truth, Bible study is, indeed, a duty and a privilege to the Christian believer; but there is a great deal of time wasted in what is called Bible study, yet which is nothing of the sort.

Philadelphia, Pa.

RIGHT SPIRIT IN BIBLE STUDY

RIGHT SPIRIT IN BIBLE STUDY

BY PROFESSOR AUSTIN PHELPS, D.D.

An astronomer was once exploring, on a clear night, the surface of the moon. His telescope, as he thought, was in perfect order. A new lens had recently been inserted in the tube. The atmosphere was clear; not a cloud was to be seen. Almost with the naked eye he could see the moon's mountains and valleys. With his splendid lens he hoped to make discoveries not seen by any astronomer before him. He was not at the first disappointed. He distinctly saw living inhabitants in the moon. He rubbed his eyes with astonishment, and again gazed, and gazed again, with trembling rapture. He certainly saw moving creatures walking with gigantic strides over the valleys and the mountains. At last the mystery was solved. One side of his new lens had not been cleansed. Upon it were a few infinitesimal insects, which, magnified by the glass to his eye, looked like strange animals, unlike any known to the natural history of earth. When the lens was rubbed clean, the strange animals vanished, and he saw no more on the moon's surface than he had seen aforetime. So much depends, in scientific discovery, on the condition of the medium one looks through, and its freedom from things foreign to the objects it was made for.

The same principle holds good in the study of the Word of God. An investigator of the Bible often sees what is not there, and as often fails to see that which is there, through some subtle defect in the spirit or the methods which he brings with him to his work. Grave errors are foisted into the sacred pages, and hidden truths remain hidden, for the want of undistorted vision in the looker-on. How, then, may such failures in the study of the Bible be avoided? A few principles deserve mention, which, for the most, lie *back of* the study itself.

1. We need to bring to the Bible *a predisposition to believe it.* The existence of such a book presupposes faith. Men are made to be believers of something, not doubters of everything. This book is God's tribute to the believing spirit with which he has endowed the soul of every man. Faith itself is a vigorous, life-like thing. It betokens vital force. We may better believe a falsehood, if it be a great one, and, so far as a falsehood can be, a pure one, than to believe nothing. Some heathen systems of religion are vastly better than nothing. He is a weakling who is a universal skeptic. To make a full-grown man of him, he needs to recover a faculty

which he has lost. To this faculty of faith the Bible makes appeal. No man is likely to discover its true meaning if he comes to it predisposed to doubt and cavil and deny. He is the very man to see monsters in his telescope. His lens is not clean and clear.

2. We need to come to the Bible *in the spirit of learners desiring to be taught.* We must come as inquirers. The book is a revelation, or it is nothing. God speaks in it, or nobody speaks who deserves a hearing. Men often flounder in unfathomed depths, in their soundings of divine truth, because they are bent on making the Scriptures what they ought to be, instead of simply asking what they are.

Suppose that God were now to speak to us in any other form of revelation. Suppose that we heard him speaking audibly from the mountains, or saw him writing his words in flame on the sky, and that we believed that. Should we not listen in awestruck silence? Should we venture to correct the voices, or revise the records? Should we dare to do any other than reverently to ask, "What is this which God is saying to us?" Yet this Bible comes to us with just such authority. It speaks to us on the assumption that we are learners, nothing more. It gives to us the privilege of inquiry, nothing else. Some portions of it have come to us literally from quaking mountains and flaming skies. The heavens have been opened, and angels of God have come down; the earth has been shaken, and men have stood in fear of their lives, to make God's thoughts clear to us. We expose ourselves to all manner of misreadings if we fail to accept this as one of the conditions of the message,—that we read as learners at the feet of a teacher, as inquirers waiting in solemn silence for God's answers.

3. It follows, therefore, that we must come to the Scriptures *as an infallible*

source of all the truth they were meant to teach. God makes no mistakes. He has never spoken of what he did not know. Scientists discover in the natural world the working of a power which is not given to blunders. We find the same in the world of revelation. This is the working of a mind which knows its own intent. It never speaks in sibylline leaves.

There are things, there are truths, great and valuable to human welfare, which the Bible is not meant to teach. On such it has no authority, and claims to have none. But on all the great moral truths on which man's salvation rests, this book is infallible. It is this or it is nothing. It speaks as one having authority. Never man spake like it. It does not offer us, as human science often does, a bundle of hypotheses. It is a book of verities. What we learn from it, we may safely say we *know.* It is not merely a possible revelation, or a probable one, to be tested by something to come after. It is a certainty, fixed and final. The world never had, and never will have, another. We need to believe this. We need to approach it, as we put our ear to a perfect telephone, assured that it will put forth no uncertain sound.

We must not come as *eclectics*, assuming to test it by our own wisdom, and to say, "This is true, and that is false; this is from God, and that is from man; here the Holy Spirit speaks, and there man blunders." Of very little worth would a revelation be of that sort. Yet a very large proportion of human errors in the reading of God's Word have arisen from this eclectic method of the reading, in which the man assumes to patch up a revelation for himself out of fragments culled here and there from the inspired pages. If we give up faith in it as an infallible revelation, we virtually give up the whole of it. God has given us no principles of interpretation by which to exercise this eclectic skill. No two men may find in the book the same revelation. That which is Bible to you may not be Bible to me.

4. From the principle just named it follows that we need to come to the Scriptures *with equal faith in the Old and the New Testaments.* The very nature and object of the volume as a revelation from God forbids the distinction men often make, to the discredit of the Old Testament. If both Testaments are not the word of God, neither is the word of God. Our chief evidence of the inspiration of the one is the word of the inspired men who made the other. One inspiring mind runs through the whole. The volume is a *structure,* in which every part is complement to every other part. Genesis and the Revelation are what Alpha and Omega are to the alphabet in which the New Testament was

written. We lose vastly of the richness and the vitality of the Old Testament if we cherish less trust in it as the word of God than we feel in the New. Then, as for the New Testament, we cannot fully understand its meaning if we do not understand the Old. Certain entire books in the two divisions are twin volumes. Each is essential to the interpretation of the other. The Epistle to the Hebrews we cannot read aright without understanding the Book of Leviticus. The Book of the Revelation needs for its interpretation the Book of Daniel. We, perhaps, think that we all of us understand the Book of Psalms; but certain of the Psalms of David were not, and could not be, fully understood till the Gospels were written. This unity of the volume as a structure, made up of interdependent parts, is a most vital principle in the true reading of it. If we ignore it, we get but a fragmentary Bible. We can only pick up here and there particles of truth, as a cannon-ball skips by *ricochet* over the surface of a lake, touching it only in spots. Is not this the practical working of much of the so-called study of the sacred books?

5. The principle just developed involves another of equal moment. It is that we must come to the Word of God *depending largely on the book itself for its own interpretation.* He is a wise man in divine knowledge who has learned to make Scripture interpret Scripture. The Bible contains a vast fund of *balanced* truths. It abounds with truths which are opposites without being contraries. One is set over against another. Thus, do we read, "God is a consuming fire"? we also read, "God is love." Are we threatened by the declaration, "God visits the iniquity of the fathers upon the children"? we turn a leaf, and are relieved by the assurance that

"the son shall *not* bear the iniquity of the father; the soul that sinneth, *it* shall die." Are we admonished that "no man *can* come unto Christ, except the Father draw him"? we are also invited: "Whosoever *will*, let him come." Are we taught "By faith ye are saved; it is the gift of God"? we are also instructed that "by works a man is justified, and not by faith only."

So the grand principles of truth are given to us as if in responsive chants, in which deep calleth unto deep. There are senses in which all these words are true. Apparent contradictions are profoundest verities. Yet we do not learn this except by allowing Scripture to interpret Scripture. Text limits text. Voice answers voice. How full the world has been of partial theologies, and how many good men have fought good men, because each heard but one of responsive voices, read but one of twin texts, and so misread the fulness of God's meaning!

It often excites our surprise that godly men and women seem so profoundly acquainted with divine things, who read little or nothing but their Bibles. We marvel that they know so much. We wonder that the mysteries of revelation disturb them so little. We are amazed that what other men call contradictions give them no trouble. What large, comprehensive souls they are! Yet this phenomenon is no matter for surprise. These godly ones are wise readers of the Word. They give it room to explain itself. They compare text with text, Gospel with Gospel, prophet with apostle, St. Peter with St. John, St. Paul with St. James; so they become very learned, even in things hard to be understood. That was a most natural prediction of President Edwards,—that "Ethiopians" might become "very knowing" in divine things. So they may, through the spirit of trust in God's Word, that it will make its own meaning clear. The deepest things of God are these balanced things, which the mind grasps in no other way than in their mysterious union, and which an illiterate mind may thus grasp as firmly as the wisest. Show me an old Bible, well thumbed, the margins of which are full of penciled references to parallel passages, and I know that it has been the comfort of some saint who became profound and comprehensive in his knowledge of the mind of God. He made discoveries which philosophers have sought for and have not found.

6. If space permitted, I would speak of the necessity of recognizing the element of *time* in the study, especially of the elder Scripture; and also of the necessity of bringing to the study a reasonable, yet not servile, respect for the *comments of learned*

men upon the Bible. But, passing these, I must hasten to speak of one other element in the spirit with which we approach the book; yet it is one which my readers will readily anticipate for themselves. It is that of *prayer for the illumination of the same Spirit who inspired the Bible.* Richard Baxter used to study the texts of his sermons on his knees. For the sake of defining to his own mind more clearly the precise object of his prayer, he would place his finger on the word of which he wanted a clearer notion, or a deeper sense, and would pray: "Lord, reveal even *this* to me; show me thy meaning!" Is it any wonder that the old church of Kidderminster was shaken by those sermons as by a mighty wind?

As a rational expedient for learning God's thought in God's Word, prayer means more than we are apt to think, when in glib phrase we commend, and, perhaps, practice it. If you had received a message from a friend, of great moment to your welfare, and if there were parts of it which you could not understand, to whom would you go for information? If you could, would you not ask that friend himself to tell you what he meant? You would ask him to put it into other language. You would ask for an illustration. If he had the power to increase your knowledge, or to lift up your mind to a level with his dark sayings, would you not ask him to do that?

Just this is the thing we do when we pray for illumination by the Holy Spirit, in our study of God's Word. We go straight to the Author of it, and ask him what he meant. We go to the Author of these minds of ours, and ask him to expand and enlighten them. We go to the Author of that grace without which spiritual knowledge is impossible, and ask him to perfect his own work within us. We seek thus to put God's work in our souls *en rapport* with God's work in the written word. There is a secret communion of the Spirit of God with our spirits, which is, in some respects, of the same nature as that of the revelation of his will in the Scriptures. This secret response of spirit to Spirit we seek to set in motion. What is more natural? None but God can know God. None but God can interpret God.

There are portions of the Bible which the ablest scholars and most devoted men are not sure that they fully understand. An eminent commentator, who is now deceased, says, in his comments on a certain text, "I must frankly confess that I do not know what this language means." The same author, with the modesty of true learning, says of other passages: "This is the *probable* meaning; with certainty I cannot speak." May it not be that these sealed pages are waiting for the wisdom of a future age to unlock them? They are, for the time, like the book which St. John saw in the Revelation of Patmos, which "no man was found worthy to open and to read." May it not be that they are waiting, not so much for the learned philologist, or the scholar most profoundly versed in Oriental research, as for an age in which Christians shall enjoy more intimate union with Christ? By bringing to the Word a deepened *experience* of the truth, the men and women of that age may be able to read aright that which now we scarcely read at all.

I have remarked that perhaps we all think we understand the Book of Psalms. Yet one of our most eminent American exegetes once said that "no man could fully understand some of them, who had not had his heart broken by some great sorrow." So there may be other treasures of divine wisdom in the deep seas of Scripture which will come up to the surface of the world's thought only at the call of some generation of Christians who shall bring to the search for them an *experience* which can spring only from much prayer and communion with God. Such knowledge of the Word the Holy Ghost may give to chosen ones whom God creates to be the world's prophets and seers. God may say to such a one what the four and twenty elders said in the new song which they sang: "Thou art *worthy* to take the book and to open the seals thereof." To such men, when their time shall come, the understanding of all parts of God's Word may be very simple.

Andover Theological Seminary.

INDUCTIVE AND DEDUCTIVE
METHODS OF STUDY

INDUCTIVE AND DEDUCTIVE METHODS OF STUDY

BY PRESIDENT ROBERT ELLIS THOMPSON, S.T.D.

We owe duties to language, which are alternatively duties to God and to our neighbor. To God we owe it to keep pure, and to wed to noble uses, the articulate speech by which we are marked as above the brute creation. To our contemporaries and to posterity we owe it to maintain that flexible permanence in the use and meaning of words which shall fit our language to convey to other minds the thoughts in which we and they find communion, and which shall transmit to coming ages the best heritage of ideas and truths that God has enabled us to attain. It is the sense of this which underlies the scholar's sensitiveness as to the right use of words, and his impatience with the innovations effected by slang or ignorance in their employment. He realizes with Luther that words are not dead things, but have a vitality of their own, which gives them a claim to the tenderness, the courtesy, the respect, of all who have to use them.

Both in biblical study and in other branches of investigation, the terms "inductive" and "deductive" are used to describe a difference in the method of getting at truth, but not always with a just sense of their meaning. They are correlative terms, and therefore neither of them is quite intelligible until we know the meaning of the other.

Deduction is the method especially of mathematical science. Geometry, for instance, sets out with a few simple statements of self-evident truths. From these it proceeds by inevitable logical steps to propositions more and more complex, until the student finds himself facing such theorems as that the shortest distance between two points on the surface of a sphere is an are of that circle which has the same center and radius as the sphere. This and every other proposition in the science of geometry lies implicit in the axioms and definitions which are printed at the beginning of every treatise on the subject, and which are so simple that to the beginner they seem almost childish.

But this kind of reasoning is confined to a very few branches of knowledge, and, indeed, it hardly can be applied with rigor outside of mathematics and their practical applications in terrestrial and celestial mechanics. There is something like the process in ethics, where certain conceptions of right and duty are given us in our intuitions, with an authority independent of experience, and thus are known to be equally true in every part of the universe. From these axiomatic truths, though with less logical rigidity, are derived more complex ethical statements in closer relation to actual life. So again, in theology, while some theologians hold that all we know of God is obtained through the study of the Scriptures, others assert that either all men, or some enlightened individuals of the races, have an immediate and intuitive knowledge of God and of divine things. On the latter hypothesis, the deductive method may be used in proceeding from these simple elements of divine knowledge to others more complex.

Induction, on the other hand, is the method chiefly employed in the so-called sciences of observation,—geology, chemistry, physics, etc. People here begin with facts and end with laws; begin with the complex and end with the simple. These sciences do not possess the high degree of certainty which attaches to mathematics, where the deductive method applies. That twice two makes four on the surface of the planet Jupiter admits of no doubt in any unsophisticated mind, whatever Professor Huxley may say. That hydrogen and oxygen will combine in equal molecular masses to form water in Jupiter, as well as here, is highly probable, but not so certain.

It is necessary to emphasize the fact that there is no such thing as getting at any law or truth by mere induction, as was assumed by the school of John Locke. Mere sense-perception would give us the facts, as it gives them to the dog, and would carry us no farther. As Coleridge says, we must bring to the facts the light in which we see them, if we are to make anything of them. No great discovery ever was made by the inductive process. Newton did not discover the law of gravitation by observing the fall of an apple, as Voltaire would have us believe ; nor did Harvey discover the circulation of the blood by mere observation, as he tells us himself. In both cases it was the outgoing of the imagination beyond the bounds of the seen and the known, which furnished the idea. Induction, however, served to *verify* the conception when it had been reached. And this, in fact, is the humble but very useful function of the inductive method. It finds nothing that is really new. To do that belongs, as Tyndall says, to " the scientific uses of the imagination." To verify and establish, to discriminate between an empty fancy and a well-founded idea, is the business of induction.

The rigorous application of the inductive method to the study of literature generally, and of the Bible in particular, would mean that the student is to divest himself

INDUCTIVE AND DEDUCTIVE STUDY 43

of all prepossessions and prejudices, and to try to find exactly what the facts stand for. He is to come to Homer with his mind free from the previous estimates of the poet, and interpretations of his poem, and to see what he himself would make of it, if he never had seen or heard of the poem before. So he is to come to the Bible with no theory of inspiration in his mind, no religious associations embarrassing his judgment, and deal with the book as though he had got it into his hands for the first time, and had never heard of its existence. This is the rigid and thorough sense of the word "induction." But, of course, no such process can be applied to the great books of the world's literature by any scholar of Europe or America. The man best situated for such a proceeding would be one of Dr. John G. Paton's converts in the South Sea Islands; but nobody supposes that his entire freedom from prepossessions would give him a more favorable position for understanding the book than Dr. Paton himself, with his Scotch nativity and schooling, and his Covenanter training, possesses. Neither Homer nor the Bible can be studied in any such fashion.

It is not in this rigid sense that the intelligent advocates of the inductive study of the Bible insist on that method. What they mean is, that this branch of study has the right to occupy a position independent of the conclusions of other branches of theology. Take the parallel case of church history. Up to the beginning of the eighteenth century, church history was "the handmaid of dogmatic theology." But in 1699-1700, Gottfried Arnold published his "Church and Heresy History," in which he revolted from this, and used church history for an attack on dogmatic theology, contending that the heretics almost always had been the real Christians, and the orthodox had been the world. In spite of his extravagances, the book introduced a new era in treating its subject. It emancipated church history; and from that time those who wrote on this theme—with the exception of a few second-rate writers like Dean Milner—concerned themselves to ascertain and state the facts, whether they were orthodox and edifying or the reverse. And, in the long run, church history has become more edifying, and the cause of true Christianity has benefited greatly by the change.

As in historical so in exegetical theology. The exposition of the Scriptures was long subject to the authority of dogmatic theology. The theory of inspiration which the latter enunciated bound the expositor to find nothing in the Bible that was inconsistent with it. The proof-texts it alleged in support of specific doctrines must not be interpreted as meaning less or more than the sense thus put upon them. If one opened a commentary on Romans by an Arminian, or a commentary on James by a Lutheran, it was not to find whether he differed from his school as to the meaning of Paul on foreordination or James on good works, but how he overcame the difficulty presented by his text, and brought it into harmony with his system. So Andreas Osiander, in his "Harmony of the Gospels," sooner than admit the slightest discrepancy between two Gospels in their accounts of the same incident, and thus imperil his theory of inspiration, treated the two accounts as narratives of different occurrences.

It is therefore the independence of exegetical study that the advocates of the inductive method are seeking to establish. They want the student to come to the Bible with an open mind, not having concluded beforehand what kind of a Bible God must have given us, if he gave us any, nor prepared to stretch and twist its statements to bring them into harmony with a dogmatic system. They do not mean, I presume, that the Bible is to be taken in hand without any prepossessions. To do so would be to ignore a large part of the facts which the exegete has to account for, — such as the vast influence for good this collection of books has exerted, and is still exerting, upon the spiritual destinies of mankind.

Those who have a real faith in the Bible are not to be disconcerted by this claim of an independent position for exegetical study. They even may expect that the first movement to liberty will take the unhappy shape of revolt against conclusions which sober second thought will re-establish on a firmer basis than the old exegesis did or could. Gottfried Arnold's handling of church history has its parallel in the results reached by some modern handling of the Scriptures. A sane exegesis always will recognize the fact that the expositor's business is not to "pick holes" in the Scriptures, but to explain the wonderful power they have exerted over the minds, affections, and characters of men.

Philadelphia, Pa.

STUDYING THE BIBLE BOOK BY BOOK

STUDYING THE BIBLE BOOK BY BOOK

BY PROFESSOR F. K. SANDERS, PH.D.

There is no royal road to the mastery of the Bible. To acquire a grasp, at once comprehensive and detailed, of its facts and teachings, an intimate friendship with its heroes and saints, an understanding of the outward conditions of its development, and an appreciation of its divine reality, is a serious task which calls for years of patient, well-directed study. There is a compensation, however, for those who look with dismay at so lengthened an effort. One may not succeed in acquiring the title to biblical scholarship, and yet may have accomplished results not merely satisfying, but valuable.

That the Bible is pre-eminently a layman's book, which richly rewards any one who gives to it earnest, thoughtful, methodical study, is clear, from several facts. The Bible is a literature, the record of actual experience, and the one who studies it is studying life. It is the history, in varied form, of man's acquirement of a true knowledge of the living God. It is a mirror in which the student may behold his own spiritual experiences enlarged and defined. The study of the Scriptures is not, therefore, a study of technicalities either of theology or of literature, but a survey of that kind of history which quickens and broadens the mind and soul of man. Every one may appropriate this in some degree, in proportion to his mastery of the facts as recorded and to his receptive power.

Again, some of the finest Bible students have been those who could study but a few minutes at a time. A busy housekeeper or a hard-working farmer may be a walking commentary, capable of expositions of biblical truth which a pastor would envy. The most fruitful Bible study is that which allows much time for meditation and review, and adjustment of new material to old.

In the third place the Bible student is not obliged to spend months or years in preliminary study before he is able to gain inspiration from his work. He will never reach a point of view which will seem to him absolutely satisfying. The more time he puts upon the study of the Bible, the more he will crave. But from the very beginning of his earnest study, he will gain suggestions which are new, stimulating, and helpful to him as a man who acknowledges his obligations to God and the universe, and seeks the aid of divine wisdom in fulfilling them.

But while no one need be turned aside from Bible study because he cannot give to it all his energy, and while he will find it fruitful from the very start, it by no means follows that earnestness is the chief requisite for success. Two other conditions must be met,—perseverance and method. The greatest danger to which the student of the Bible is exposed is the temptation to demand results prematurely. In spiritual life, as well as in agriculture, the choicest fruits require time and care for their ripening.

There is no such thing as a clear-cut method of Bible study which will apply to all students and on every occasion. Every true student will, in the course of time, adopt peculiarities of method which are developed by attention to that class of results which he particularly values. It is, however, possible to suggest certain principles which underlie all successful study, and to indicate a practicable method of applying them.

The first of these principles is based upon

the fact that the Bible, as we have it, is a noble literature. We cannot study a book of the Bible without recognizing to some degree its literary form and grouping. A historical work like the books of Kings or Samuel should be approached in a way quite distinct from that adopted for the study of a collection of detached utterances like the Psalter or the Book of Proverbs, of a carefully finished production such as the Book of Job, or of an impassioned, many-sided line of thought such as we find in an epistle or a prophetic book. The first step to be taken after a book has been selected for study is to note its general character and to determine the method of its mastery.

A principle of equal importance is based upon the distractions of the average student's daily life. The best way of mastering the whole Bible is to master one book at a time. It makes comparatively little difference what book is selected, for the careful study of one will lead the way to the study of those most closely related to it, and thus to the study of all. The majority of people must make Bible study of this sort an avocation to which they may be able to devote at the utmost a few hours a week; their duties as teachers in the Sunday-school, or as members of the church, consume the chief part of their spare time. Truly remarkable results, however, can be gained by the devotion of a little time, week by week, to one single line of effort.

It is insufficient to merely read this book. Reading conduces to a certain kind of familiarity, very valuable in its way, yet remote from mastery. It is an excellent preliminary, but no more. One who aims to read the Bible through, from cover to cover, once a year, may be no nearer to becoming a biblical scholar than the boy who rattles off the multiplication-table is to becoming a mathematician. It depends, in each case, on what they do next.

The basis for the exact and fruitful study of any biblical book must always be a grasp of its course of thought as outlined in the book itself. This defines and reinforces the impression produced by reading, and affords a safe starting-point for investigation. The test to be applied at this stage of the work is the ability to think through the book, and compare paragraph with paragraph without referring to the Bible. It is enough at first to be able to do this by sections of thought.

The last principle that need be mentioned is a comprehensive one. When one has gained a hold upon the contents of a book, he should study it from every possible point of view,—its relation to other biblical books, its contribution to various biblical problems, its literary form and structure, its religious content, the element of revelation, or other interesting questions, determined by experience or special purpose. This will be a never-ending pleasure, for, as one's knowledge of the Bible increases, new points of view suggest themselves for investigation and comparison.

It remains to give a practical illustration of the application of these principles. This can only be done in a very general, and perhaps unsatisfactory, way. It will serve, however, as a guide to one who is desirous of taking up some serious study of the Bible for himself. It is probable that such a one will wish to begin with a historical book, a gospel, a book of prophecy, or an epistle. It is understood that he has selected a book, not because he wishes to make an immediate use of it, but because he wishes to master it. He is not to be hurried. If necessary, he is willing to spend a year of special study upon it. The order of work suggested is only one good method, approved by its excellent results, but claiming no pre-eminence.

The first step to take is a thoughtful reading. If possible, the book should be read at a sitting, the general impression of its theme and substance thus made being considered and written down, read through at a sitting once more, the impression corrected, and so on, until a fairly well defined notion of the book as a whole has been formed. The nature of the impression expected will vary with the book selected. In a history, one might determine the point of view of the compiler; in a gospel, the "leading ideas;" in an epistle, the "key-note." In each case the student would record no more than his impression.

The next step is to correct or extend this impression by considering a logical arrangement of the contents of the book. Many analyses will be available in Bible helps, commentaries, etc. The impression previously gained by the careful reading will enable the student to select that analysis which most nearly recognizes it. If such an analysis can be found, it will best serve his purpose. If he finds none especially suitable, any analysis will do, a preference being suggested for one that merely aims to logically correlate the contents. Such are usually found in the commentaries of the Cambridge Bible series. For many New Testament books some excellent analyses have been published, within a year or two, in the Biblical World (University of Chicago).

The usefulness of an analysis lies in its indication of the logical relations of the different sections of the contents of a book. It is an excellent guide in mastering the contents—no more. It is not wise to commit an analysis to memory until one is convinced that it exactly represents his own ripest thought. It is a convenient intellectual crutch, to be gradually disused or exchanged for something better.

Guided by the analysis adopted, the student should take up the mastery of the contents of the book, section by section. He should aim to get at the thought of each section, *and to get at all of it.* Reading will not accomplish this, for the reader unconsciously ignores much of his text. The only sure way of accomplishing it is to make a paraphrase in case of a connected train of thought, as in an epistle or a prophetic book, or to make a condensed summary of the facts in case one is studying a historical book or a gospel. The student is thus forced to determine with exactness what a paragraph contains. An example or two may be helpful. They are taken at random.

"Listen, all of you! What an unheard-of and memorable calamity has come upon us! The greedy, numerous, swift, and destructive locust, swarm after swarm, has utterly devoured the land. Mourn, ye drinkers of wine, for your source of supply is gone. This invading swarm, as strong and numberless as an army, as fierce and destructive as a lion, has stripped the vines and fig trees of foliage, and left them whitening in the sun" (Joel 1 : 1-7). "I never fail to give thanks to God in my prayers for your well-rounded Christian character and experience; for I know that you were never contented with listening to the gospel message, but strove to act in its spirit, obtaining help from the example of Christ, and of me, your teacher. You have been a great help to the work of preaching, not only in Macedonia and in Greece, but everywhere, because of your hearty and thorough-going rejection of idolatry and your service of God, to which you were encouraged by the redemption which is offered through Jesus" (1 Thess. 1 : 2-10).

STUDYING BOOK BY BOOK   63

A paraphrase of this sort is not difficult after a little practice. It merely reproduces the biblical statements in plain language, but in the spirit and form of the original passage. It compels the student to interpret, as well as read, with exactness. In a similar way, the statements or the narrative of a gospel or historical book should be summarized, section by section.

After a book has been mastered in detail in this way, the student should correct his analysis. He is now in a position to make an analysis of his own, one based upon the contents as he interprets them, and emphasizing the leading conception which has impressed him. It is quite possible that the plain analysis, based on the simple facts, may not be the correct one, even for a historical book. First Samuel, for example, is a book which uses historical facts to set forth a religio-political theme. An analysis which fails to recognize the theme is an imperfect analysis. It must always be kept in mind, however, that the best analysis is one's own. An imperfect one of his own make is worth more to a student than any which is furnished to him. He uses the latter only that he may be able to make the former.

By this time the student has attained an excellent mastery of the book as a product of thought. He should be able to think through it at will, and to estimate it as a whole. But he is only at the threshold of his study of the book. He is ready for its topical treatment. What the topics should be depends, again, upon the book that is being studied. The following are suitable for any book: The literary structure (in which one's own plan may be compared with those found in commentaries), indications as to the author or the time of writing, information regarding the geographical, ethnological, political, social, or religious, conditions of the day, the imagery of the book, its religious teachings, etc. Any student who begins to study topically will soon make his own list of topics, and it will be far from brief. In the class-room study of the pre-exilic prophets, a few months ago, its members selected, as the work proceeded, some twenty-five distinct topics for the complete classification of the books studied. With the exception of a few very simple topics, each was selected in order to cover some facts discovered in the material. This is the true way of selecting topics. Let there be a topic for every clear-cut fact or class of facts.

When the book has been traversed again and again from many points of view, the student begins to know it in such an intimate way that he becomes a real specialist so far as it is concerned. He then is ready to take up another book in the same fashion. The Bible, thus mastered, becomes one's real property, an infinitely precious possession, a source of unlimited suggestion and of wonderful power.

The kind of study outlined above is independent study. Almost nothing has been said about "helps." These are a necessity to the one who would teach without study. They are useful to the scholar who already has ideas of his own. They are almost always a hindrance to the genuine student who is willing to work for results, but has them yet to attain.

This kind of study takes time and thought and patience, but it leads to solid results. It may seem to place too much stress on mere verbal details, yet it merely leads the student to determine for himself exactly what the Bible says. Only to the one who knows this, and can make use of it, does the Bible become in truth a "sword of the Spirit."

Yale University.

SCRIPTURE EXPLAINING
SCRIPTURE

SCRIPTURE EXPLAINING SCRIPTURE

BY PROFESSOR J. L. M. CURRY, D.D., LL.D.

The Sunday-school has, in one sense, exalted the Bible. In the minds of many, old and young, more than ever before since the promise of the coming of the Desire of all nations, the Bible has become *the one book*, better than all other books. Its study has increased a thousand fold. More minds engaged in exploring its mysteries, in comprehending its grand truths, in receiving its exceeding great and precious promises. Aid and appliances for its better study have been enlarged beyond the dreams of the most hopeful. The interest in the study has kept pace with and multiplied these facilities. Besides commentaries, and books of Oriental travel, and lectures, and maps, the newspaper has been a most potent auxiliary.

All these aids, however valuable, are not designed to supersede the study of the Scriptures, by comparing Scripture with Scripture, "spiritual things with spiritual." Those who teach should not fail to mark, and inwardly digest, and properly expound, the connection and harmony of divine truth as revealed in the Bible. This will tend to the building on gold and silver and precious stones instead of on hay and stubble, and to make one's faith rest upon a divine *yea, verily*, rather than on the commandments of men.

Written at different times, in different countries, by persons in different conditions of life, there is a marvelous consistency of thought and unity of doctrine. An analysis of any one book will show a purpose and scope quite remote from the scope and purpose of another book, but all the books are parts of a symmetrical whole. Systematic theology is nowhere taught. With the present constitution of the human mind it may have been impossible. Universal history is also an impossibility, but many separate treatises of widely remote men and governments, if combined, might be accurate and full. The Bible was written under different dispensations, but is progressive, culminating in Christianity, and our study of it should be like what Herodotus describes of the building of the pyramids, rising from the bottom, course by course of granite, to the marble summit, and thence finished by working downwards. Without appreciation of man's fall as narrated in Genesis we cannot appreciate Calvary, and without the Cross we cannot understand the transgression.

Probably not a single truth of much religious importance is taught in the Bible which is not repeated several times. Doubt and uncertainty in reference to a truth may be removed by looking at it in its varied relations and aspects. What may not stand out clearly in one passage, from being stated incidentally or in a condensed form, may be explained more fully in another place. The Gospels read together, or harmonized, are seen in a new light. The characteristics of the biographers of the Saviour are seen in their peculiar manner of relating the same incident or discourse. What is briefly mentioned by one will be brought out by another in minute and pictorial detail. Parallel passages, brought under view at one time, become mutually explicatory and elucidative. If the same author has related the same fact as is done in Acts, or discussed the same doctrine as is done in Romans and Galatians, obviously a comparison of the passages is the most reasonable mode of arriving at the full truth. These parallelisms are more numerous than the casual or inattentive reader would suspect. Words, phrases, passages, books, will be found reciprocally illustrative and helpful. Predictions become verifications, prophecies facts, types and symbols turn into realities.

Our International Lessons have often been too fragmentary, failing to bring into sufficient fulness an incident or a doctrine. To a modified extent, the schools have suffered the evils of textual preaching, when a sentence or a part of a sentence has been insulated, forcibly wrested from its logical connections, and made to do compulsory service in supporting a system of theology or an article of a creed, or in giving the appearance of scriptural sanction to a discourse. Words even are detached and made the basis of sermons. I once heard a man preach from the text, *Come*, and he made each letter serve for a head or division : C for conversation ; O, obedience ; M, mortality ; E, eternity. A book, a sentence, a word, by such torturing and quartering, can be made to mean or teach anything. No book but the Bible could have endured such persecution and survived.

The authors of the books in the Bible, while inspired, were yet men, and used in their communications the ordinary laws of the human mind. In seeking to present and impress facts and ideas, they sought to appeal to and use the universal laws of the mind. Every word is not a condensation of divine truth, nor has it usually a meaning distinct from its ordinary use. The writings of Isaiah, Moses, Paul, and John are to be judged and interpreted as other writings. Correlated passages should be permitted to support and throw light upon one another. To take words or thoughts out of their connection is unjust to any writer, inspired or profane. Spurgeon likes the *comes* of the Bible. Dr. Fuller rejoiced in the *shalls*. More obscure persons delight in the *therefores*, and the relational words which enforce or conclude an argument of an apostle. These hinge-words are often full of significance, and cannot, either in scholarly exercises or Sunday-school teaching, be safely ignored.

Not simply the immediate connections of a lesson should be studied, but the knowledge of the attending historical circumstances may be indispensable to an understanding of the writer's meaning. These writings, as already intimated, moreover, are not purposeless. The letters to the churches in Rome and Philippi and Corinth had not the same end in view. Each was called out by different incitements. Paul, while fond of excursions into kindred fields of thought, and often indulging in rapturous and episodic exclamations of joy and thankfulness, had consecution of thought and rare logical power. Let his statements and arguments be taken as a whole, in their comprehensiveness and fulness, and they will not be so "hard to be understood," nor so often "wrested" to mischief. To know what prompted a letter, a rebuke, an appeal, and to appreciate the personal references in a letter, are very necessary to its understanding. Errors and heresies, rife in apostolic times, have ceased to exist. Local divisions grew sometimes out of circumstances, or from causes that can have no counterpart in our day or in our country. To interpret every sentence as being a summary of the plan of salvation, or every epistle as a system of theology, is a perversion of all the rules of interpretation as well as of common sense.

The advantages of studying Scripture by Scripture will be realized when tried with a prayerful and submissive reliance upon the Holy Spirit. The Bible will not then be

SCRIPTURE EXPLAINING SCRIPTURE

such a sealed book. To read it will not be so irksome. Preparation of lessons will be increasingly a labor of love. Teaching a class will have its own reward. Scholars will find in the Scriptures more and more that is adapted to their needs and aspirings. The Word of God is a mirror perfectly revealing the nature and experiences of the soul. Persons are often deterred by ponderous or learned commentaries, who, if taught to find in Scripture an explanation of Scripture, would treasure the Book as of priceless worth. Valuable as are all the lights that science and travel and pious scholarship have thrown on the Bible, Bishop Horsley's oft-quoted words will bear another repetition, " I will not scruple to assert that the most illiterate Christian, if he can but read his English Bible, and will take the pains to read it in this manner [that is, by comparing every text with parallel passages in other parts of the Holy

Writ], will not only attain all that practical knowledge which is necessary to his salvation, but, by God's blessing, he will become learned in everything relating to his religion in such a degree that he will not be liable to be misled either by the refined arguments or the false assertions of those who endeavor to engraft their own opinions upon the oracles of God. . . . Let him study the Old and New Testament in the manner I recommend, and let him *never cease to pray for the illumination of that Spirit*, by which these books were dictated, and the whole compass of abstruse philosophy and recondite history shall furnish no argument with which the perverse will of man shall be able to shake this *learned Christian's* faith."

Richmond College, Va.

STUDY OF THE BIBLE AS LITERATURE

STUDY OF THE BIBLE AS LITERATURE

BY PROFESSOR GEORGE B. STEVENS, PH.D., D.D.

The principal value and use of the Bible will always be found in the spiritual instruction and edification which it affords. This use is most in harmony with its origin and character as a record of God's revelations, and as a proclamation of his redeeming love. This use accords with the purpose of the Bible, which is practical and religious. Its great central thoughts relate to God and man,—the nature, love, and purposes of God, and the duty and true destiny of man.

The Bible, which treats chiefly of the relations of man to God, is therefore pre-eminently the book of duty. It teaches men what God requires of them and makes possible for them. It opens to mankind the meaning of their own life. Disclosing God's thoughts for man, it teaches the dignity of human life, and enables men to discover and receive as their own the divine conception of what they should do and be. The Bible is the book of life. It is comparatively oblivious of all subjects except salvation, character, goodness. Its great lessons and truths relate to what God has done and is ever doing to save men to their best possible selves. Its chief emphasis is always upon righteousness, an inner life of harmony with God, and of growing likeness in all that is God-like.

But all these great truths are set in a historic framework. They are, in the main, not in abstract, but in concrete form. They are woven into the warp and woof of history, illustrated and enforced in the lives of individuals, communities, and nations.

They run as pervading lessons through the careers of men and peoples; they are bound up in images and similitudes, in types and symbols; they are found in letters and sermons; some of their tenderest tones breathe through poems and prayers. Thus the Bible presents to the student of it all the chief types of literary form. It must, to some extent, be studied as literature, with literary appreciation, and with reference to its literary phenomena and peculiarities, if it is to be intelligently, as well as devoutly, studied.

The religious use and the literary study of the Bible are in no way inconsistent; each should be, and may be, made very helpful to the other. The religious character and value of the Bible should make its literary study more earnest and reverent, while an appreciation of the Bible as history and literature will more fully disclose its meaning and emphasize its value.

As religion must be both intelligent and devout if it will produce the best results in character; so biblical study, which is so vitally related to religion, should both appreciate and reverently receive the spiritual truth of the Bible, and also seek to understand the forms in which it is presented, and the providential conditions and circumstances under which those truths have been revealed and the historic agencies which have been employed to this end. If these two methods of Bible study do not react helpfully upon one another, it can only be either because reverence for the Bible is blind and superstitious, or because the literary study of it is cold and unappreciative.

One of the most important aids for the better appreciation of the Bible as literature is found in the method sometimes called the "Book-study." For many purposes a piecemeal study of passages may be useful, but for anything like an intelligent knowledge of biblical literature a study of whole books in their individual character and unity is most important.

Particularly is this true of the epistles and prophecies, which have, generally speaking, a closer unity than historical books which combine a great variety of matter. One might be much profited by a study of selected passages of the Epistle to the Romans, in which each passage was studied for its own sake and without special reference to its connections or the purpose of the Epistle as a whole, but he could never gain a comprehensive knowledge or intelligent appreciation of the Epistle as a whole by such a study. Moreover, he could not gain even a correct apprehension of any of its parts without viewing them in their relation to the purpose and scope of the Epistle as a whole. This is one reason why the popular exposition of Scripture is often so crude and violent.

Let us suppose that an interested student wished to secure for himself an intelligent and appreciative acquaintance with Latin literature. He might request some competent person to select for him certain passages of chief beauty and importance in Virgil, Cicero, Tacitus, and the other leading writers. Upon these he might bestow painstaking attention, examining every word and mastering each idea. He might gain thus a considerable knowledge of the literature, but never a mastery of it in this method. These fragments are but parts of a unified whole. They are elements of a structure. No knowledge of the elements as such can give us an appreciation of the structure as a whole; and without this, we cannot even fully appreciate the parts which compose it.

I am convinced that, along with the excellent movement now making in the Christian world to promote thorough, painstaking, and minute study of passages, there ought to be a corresponding popular movement in the direction of a comprehensive knowledge of the Bible as history and literature which should enable Christian people to get a clearer and stronger grasp upon biblical books as a whole, and aid to a better understanding of the peculiarities, aims, and scope of various books and groups of books in that great body of sacred literature which we call the Bible.

I would not in the least depreciate the tendency to minuteness in the study of selected passages; the knowledge which such study can yield is indispensable; but it cannot have its best value and use if it is secured at the expense of a comprehensive view of the whole field of biblical history and literature, which alone can co-ordinate and unify individual texts and their details. Microscopy is an important science, but its exclusive pursuit would never yield a just view of the universe.

The more general conviction that each and every passage is sacred Scripture, and is given for our instruction, is by no means enough to enable us to make the use of it for which it was intended. One must know in the line of what thought and purpose the passage is, before he can rightly judge what it is meant to teach. Without recognizing this principle, the words of Scripture become subject to all sorts of false conjuring.

For the appreciation of the Bible as literature, attention must also be given to the peculiarities of individual authors, and to the different types of thought and writing. It is an absolute prerequisite to a just apprehension of the New Testament, not only to know in what fundamental respects Matthew differs from Luke, the three Synoptists from John, Romans from Corinthians, Thessalonians from Philippians, etc., but to know in what respects the Pauline type of teaching and modes of thought differ from those of Peter and James.

Such points cannot be determined in one's own study except by close examination. Not many have leisure or adaptation for their pursuit; they should, in such cases, be ascertained at second hand from some competent authority, and carried into the study of biblical books and passages as guiding lights. Such information would serve as a clew to guide many a reader into an intelligent understanding of books which now seem only a confused jumble. When one knows the chief aim and guiding thought of a book, together with something of the peculiarities, conditions, and character of the writer, even though he derive all this information from another, he has a key to the book which can unlock its meaning as no mere study of isolated passages could ever do. In possession of this, he can test and verify by careful and continuous study the theory of the book, or group of books, and can intelligently make his own a view of their scope and contents as a whole, and of the relations of all the parts to that whole.

This method of study has given rise to the comparatively new science of biblical theology. Its application is, to a considerable extent, practicable for non-professional Bible students. How important to understand the chief characteristics of the Pauline or the Johannine writings! What new light a knowledge of these peculiarities casts upon many of their expressions and conceptions! Without some such appreciation of their ruling ideas, much that they have written appears to the reader confused and meaningless. The importance of what I am urging is often overlooked and disparaged by those who are lacking in the "historic sense" as applied to the Scriptures; who assume that, because the Scriptures are given for all people and all times, that, therefore, they can be understood by all earnest people in all times without a study of the times in which they were produced or the peculiarities and special aims of those who were the human instruments of their composition.

There is, of course, a certain truth in this view. But one should distinguish between that practical knowledge of what the Scriptures teach as duty, and that more comprehensive knowledge which, while including this, goes beyond it, and seeks to determine the forms and channels through which God, in ancient times, has been pleased to make known his will. Selected passages could easily be culled out which would sufficiently show the path of duty and the principles of life, but the Bible is not a mere text-book: it is history and literature, and if we will study it for what it is, we must study it in its character as history and literature, as well as in that of spiritual guide and manual of morals.

Intelligent study of the Bible has often been discountenanced by the assurance that the Bible is easy. In this view there is also contained the truth that it is easy to learn from the Bible what God requires us to do and to become; but the statement that the Bible is easy to understand is misleading and false, if it mean either that it is easy for the human mind to comprehend the full meaning and depth of the most obvious truths of Scripture, or that it does not require, and in some cases even overtaxes the profoundest study to determine the intention and significance of many parts of the Scriptures. Peter did not seem to share the opinion and experience of those who find the Scriptures so easy; certainly he did not respecting the epistles of Paul, "wherein are some things hard to be understood" (2 Pet. 3 : 16).

The truth is that for a right appreciation even of the ethical and practical portions of Scripture, intelligent and diligent study is necessary. I emphasize the word "intelligent;" for there is a great deal of diligent Bible study which is not intelligent, and which therefore goes oftener wrong than right in interpretation, even if it does not wholly misconceive and pervert the intention and spirit of the passages handled. Discrimination of things that differ, perception of the relations of ideas, the avoidance of misplaced and exaggerated emphasis, and some knowledge of the times and conditions to which the passage under consideration relates, are some of the marks of intelligent study.

It is not unimportant to recognize and appreciate the different kinds of literature which find place in the Bible. We have history in the forms of narrative, chronicle, and biography ; we have letters addressed to churches, groups of churches, and to individuals; we have orations and sermons; we have fiction in the parables of the Old Testament and the New, and in the drama of the Book of Job; we have poetry of the loftiest character in the psalms and some of the prophets, a dramatic poem in the Song of Songs, and a prose pastoral in Ruth; besides these, we have proverbs, codes of law, ethical treatises, prayers, elegies, and narratives of visions. For the student of literature, here is abundant and various material.

But with this variety there is combined a unity of spirit which imparts a unique character to the whole. It is not strange that educators are asking whether this literature should not have place in a curriculum of liberal study, and whether we have not overlooked the value for culture of this body of literature, which is widely known and read, but which, nevertheless, is less studied and understood, as literature, by intelligent and well-informed people, than any other of even approximate proportions, interest, and availability.

The value of knowing, so far as possible, the immediate, specific aims with which the various books were written, cannot easily be overestimated. This is especially true of the epistles of Paul. To know something of the churches to which they were addressed, of the occasion which called them forth, of the dangers in doctrine or in life against which they were designed to guard the Christian communities, and of the specific misconceptions of the gospel which they were in some cases intended to correct, is absolutely essential to an intelligent reading of their contents. Without some knowledge of this kind, one can no more rightly understand some of these epistles than he could appreciate the force and point of " In Memoriam," while knowing nothing of Tennyson's friend whom it commemorates, or of his character, relations to the family of the poet, or the circumstances of his death. There might be a limited appreciation of the poem without this, but severely limited it would be.

It will be a great gain to the cause of theology and religion when the Bible is more studied and understood as literature. In this way, truer conceptions of what the Bible is will come to prevail. When the historical relations and literary forms with which its truths and teachings are inseparably connected are better appreciated, its true meaning and value will be more apparent, interpretations which defy philology and history alike will be less frequent and persistent, and the possibility of a far better agreement among Christians respecting the essentials of faith will be founded.

Yale University.

HINTS AS TO BIBLE INTERPRETATION

HINTS AS TO BIBLE INTERPRETATION

BY PRESIDENT JOHN A. BROADUS, D.D., LL.D.

A good many teachers who have no opportunity, or no inclination, to read elaborate treatises on the interpretation of the Bible, may be willing to look through some homely suggestions.

1. Be willing to let the Bible mean what it wants to mean. If you think that is a matter of course, I cannot agree with you. All of us who teach Bible lessons have certain doctrinal views, certain established prepossessions, certain constitutional tendencies to prefer this or that way of regarding and presenting any point of religious truth. It is doubtful whether any one of us ever does approach a Scripture

lesson with entire willingness that it shall mean what it wishes to mean. But assuredly we ought to make earnest effort in this direction. We reproach a politician who labors to explain the Constitution in some unnatural way to suit himself, a lawyer who deals likewise with the language he is reading from a law book, a business man who perverts the terms of a written contract; but still more blameworthy are we, if we know beforehand what we want this passage to mean, and then put screws to it that it may be forced into suiting our views and wishes. Here is a grave fault, and if everybody is tempted to commit the fault, then we ought to make earnest and prayerful efforts to form the habit of submitting our preferences to the real meaning of the inspired Book we are undertaking to interpret.

2. Give careful attention to the connection of your passage. Not only does every

sentence of the lesson usually have some distinct connection with the rest, but the lesson as a whole has its connection with what precedes and follows. One of the gravest and commonest faults among Sunday-school teachers and pupils consists in treating the lesson as an independent whole, without regard to its connection in the book and in the Bible. The lesson is printed separately, and multitudes of pupils, with a large proportion of teachers, will never stop to think of what has gone before. But even with the Bible before one's eyes, there is a grievous tendency to indolent neglect of the connection. This has been fostered by the common fashion of printing the Bible without distinct indication of paragraphs, such as we have in all other books, and with every scrap of a verse printed as if itself a paragraph, when it may be only part of a sentence.

Ministers also have in many cases done

great mischief, in this respect, by taking a short text because easily remembered, and then interpreting its language in any way that seems to yield helpful ideas, and regarding it as a sort of bondage to keep within the limits of the connection. Many years ago, a wise father gave his little boy a simple lesson, which has never been forgotten. He said, "I can prove to you out of the Bible that there is no God." So the boy brought a Bible, which the father opened, and, placing his finger over some words, bade him read. There it was, beginning with a capital letter, like a complete sentence, "There is no God." The child stared; but when the finger was lifted, it read, "The fool hath said in his heart, There is no God." You may say that, of course, no one would so utterly and flagrantly disregard the connection as in that case. But, suffer a person who has given much attention to teaching and preaching and commentary, to say that, in hundreds, if not thousands, of cases, he has seen the connection disregarded, not so obviously, perhaps, but in a fashion just as real and just as misleading.

The connection of a lesson may be only a few preceding and following sentences, or a chapter or two. In a higher and very real sense, the lesson stands in relation to the whole book of which it forms a part, and cannot be precisely and soundly interpreted without reference to the general contents and aim of that entire book. In one sense, the connection is the whole Bible.

3. Remember that the Bible is a very old book. If you read Homer or the "Arabian Nights," if you examine sentences which were inscribed thousands of years ago on some monument in Egypt or in Mesopotamia, you would not expect every word to mean there precisely what

the same word would mean in the morning newspaper. Even when scholars have made you a translation, the words have a different setting,—carry with them a different atmosphere. You need to remember that this was written a long time ago, far away from here, among a people whose ideas and favorite expressions were in some respects quite peculiar, or, at any rate, quite different from my own.

Now as to the main substance of the numerous and distinct books which we recognize as inspired, they appeal very strikingly to those elements of human nature and conditions of human thought and action which are essentially universal and unchangeable. But as to the details of conception and expression, as to the precise color and tone, these books often differ very widely from what the same words would mean in a writing of to day. We have all insensibly learned something in this respect from life-long familiarity with at least the surface of the inspired Word, and from the extent to which its modes of thought and expression have pervaded all the preaching and teaching and religious literature to which our attention has been directed. But much remains to be done, and done with persistent and painstaking effort, by one who wishes to interpret the Bible safely. Remember that it abounds in terms and phrases which carry a meaning of their own, quite different from the sense in which similar phrases and terms would be employed in a current newspaper.

4. Compare Scripture with other portions of Scripture. Much help is given for this by the reference Bibles, the lesson-helps, and the commentaries. It may be a very profitable exercise, but it is often so managed as to be highly misleading. Some other passage may contain the same term or phrase that you are dealing with ;

but it may there convey quite a different sense, as a careful consideration of the connection in that case would show.

If you jump at the conclusion that such a word as "soul" or "righteousness" or "hell" means the same thing in every passage, you will be gravely mistaken, and your comparison of passages will do more harm than good. So if you find that essentially the same subject is treated in another passage, it may yet be there presented in quite a different light, and the difference requires attention. The use of a reference Bible may thus range all the way from the laziest to the most laborious method of Bible study.

5. Interpret the Bible upon principles of common sense. Recognizing and keeping in mind the peculiar range of thought and usage of language which mark the sacred writings, we yet cannot fail to see that they appeal constantly to the plain

good sense of a thoughtful and sober mind. Some commentators and ministers think they put honor upon the Bible by making a certain expression mean several different things at the same time,—things which are hopelessly incompatible and mutually exclusive. That is not sensible. Some insist on the literal meaning of what is plainly a figure of speech.

One day some gentlemen were looking at certain huge stones in the southwest corner of the Haran enclosure at Jerusalem, which evidently formed a part of the wall in Herod's time. "What would you say then," inquired one of the party, "as to the statement that 'there shall not be one stone left upon another, but all shall be cast down'?" "I should say," was the reply, "that the author of that statement expected people to have some sense."

6. Cultivate spiritual sympathy with the Bible; for it is a spiritual book. It is full

of rich historical color, it abounds in curious facts and striking characters, and has an immense wealth of allusion to phenomena of nature and of human life ; but all is pervaded by a supreme and controlling spirituality. Persons utterly destitute of spirituality often sadly fail to understand, and some can even ridicule, when, if they had proper spiritual sympathies, they would as soon think of ridiculing their mother's last words on her dying-bed. Other things are very desirable for a just interpretation of Scripture. Spiritual sympathies, genuine and ever freshly cherished, are indispensable.

Southern Baptist Theological Seminary.

NEED OF ORIENTAL LIGHTS
ON THE BIBLE

NEED OF ORIENTAL LIGHTS ON THE BIBLE

BY H. CLAY TRUMBULL, D.D.

It is obvious that he who would understand the Bible as containing a message of God, needs to know the meaning of its words and phrases and figures of speech; for, if he lacks such knowledge, its more important truths will surely be hidden from him. It is not enough to say that God, while sending a vitally important message to common people, must have seen to it that it was given in language which all could understand alike, while taking the words in their natural and simplest meaning. What of God's ways with men?

Even the best blessings from God require effort on man's part to make them available for his welfare. When the sunlight comes from the heavens, a man must open his eyes to it, or it will not give light to him. If manna falls to the earth for his daily food, he must gather it piece by piece, and carefully prepare it for eating, and then eat it as though it had been an ordinary growth in the harvest field, or he will as certainly starve as if God had never sent such food for his sustenance. God forces his best blessings on none. He proffers them to all who are willing to make them available.

Men have to learn human language before they can understand human language. And not all men understand the same language. The Bible was originally written in Hebrew, and Chaldaic, and Greek, and already it has been translated from those languages into more than two hundred other languages and dialects, and even yet not all the human race is provided for. All the separate books of the Bible were written in the East, primarily for those who were trained in the East under Oriental influences and methods and customs. Many of the figures of speech employed in the Bible as simple and intelligible to those for whom it was first written, now require explanation in order to be understood by those who have been trained in other parts of the world in later times, and under new conditions of life.

When, for instance, we read in the Bible that in the dark days of adversity there shall no longer be heard in the city streets "the voice of the bridegroom and the voice of the bride" (Jer. 7 : 34; 16 : 9; 25 : 10; 33 : 11; Rev. 18 : 23), we have nothing in our occidental experiences to explain this common figure of speech. Bridegrooms and brides, in our Western civilization, are not accustomed to cry or shout in the city streets, so long as they live peaceably with one another. But when we learn that both the bride and the bridegroom in Oriental countries are accompanied through the city streets by separate processions before they are married, and that hardly any event in Eastern social life is the occasion of such hilarity, or of such riotous rejoicing, as a marriage ceremony, we gain a fresh understanding of the force of the Bible illustration.

Similarly, the words of John the Baptist concerning his delight in the welcome given to Jesus as the Messiah are meaningless without an explanation of their Oriental significance. "He that hath the bride is the bridegroom: but the friend of the bridegroom, which standeth and heareth him, rejoiceth greatly because of the bridegroom's voice: this my joy therefore is fulfilled. He must increase, but I must decrease" (John 3 : 29, 30). In the East, the bridegroom does not see his bride before their marriage. "The friend of the bridegroom" arranges the match. When the bridegroom meets the bride, if he is satisfied he communicates the fact to those who are waiting without. Their cry of rejoicing informs the friend of the bridegroom, and gratifies him by the knowledge that he has done well his part. John the Baptist had prepared the way for the coming of the Bridegroom Jesus to his Bride, the Church. When he found that delight followed that union he was glad to know that *his* mission was accomplished.

When, again, we find that Jesus, in sending out his disciples by two and two, told them to "take nothing for their journey, save a staff only; no bread, no wallet, no money in their purse," as if they were to be miraculously supported in their evangelistic tours (Matt. 10 : 1-10 ; Mark 6 : 7-9; Luke 9 : 2-4), we fail to comprehend the naturalness of the suggestions, unless we are made acquainted with the prevalence of the spirit of hospitality in the East. Then we realize that any Oriental who throws himself on the hospitality of others as he journeys is sure of a welcome; and we perceive that this fact throws light on many a reference in the Bible to social customs and duties otherwise inexplicable.

So simple an expression as "man goeth to his long home, and the mourners go about the streets" (Eccl. 12 : 5) fails to convey its full meaning to one who knows nothing of Oriental mourning customs. An ordinary reader might, indeed, suppose that the expression merely pointed out the fact that when a man is dead his companions soon return to their ordinary occupations, as though nothing of importance had happened among them. But a familiarity with the East shows one that when a person dies his friends at once begin their noisy wailing, and that all who hear it take up the cry and repeat it vociferously; that mourners, professional or sympathetic, go through the neighboring streets with loud wails, beating their breasts, and burdening the air with doleful cries. In view of such customs, understood by the reader, the Bible references to death and mourning have a vividness and meaning not secured to those who lack this knowledge.

It is thus at many a point in the Bible text. Unless one understands the importance of the position of a guardian of the threshold in an ancient temple, or knows how high an honor is esteemed the post of keeper or protector of the royal palace entrance, he is liable to misconceive or to misinterpret the true meaning of the Psalmist's words when he says proudly, not in obsequious humility, " I had rather be a doorkeeper in [or, stand at the threshold of] the house of my God, than to dwell in the tents of wickedness" (Psa. 84 : 10).

Again, until we know of the primitive

lamps in use in the East in Bible times, where, in an open receiver of oil or melted tallow, a simple linen rag, or rude wick of flax, furnished its dim light to one who kept that flax in flame, and the receiver supplied with oil, we are incapable of seeing the force of many a Bible phrase which otherwise gives light to the open mind. "The smoking flax shall he not quench" (Isa. 42 : 3 ; Matt. 12 : 20) tells with peculiar force of the tender, patient love of the Messiah, when it is seen that it means that he will even revive a dimly burning wick which otherwise would expire.

Even different parts of the great East need explanations from the customs of other parts in order to make clear and forcible many figures of speech which were bright as sunlight to those to whom they were first spoken in the Bible pages. Canon Tristram of Durham gives a vivid illustration of this truth out of his varied experiences of travel. He is unusually familiar with Palestine and its customs, and the Bible figures of that region speak to him with exceptional force. Being in Ceylon while on a journey around the world, he preached one day, through an interpreter, to a congregation of native Christians whom he longed to help. He took the familiar figure of the Good Shepherd, and presented it in its simplicity as a lesson about Jesus in his loving care of his people.

When the service was over, the perplexed interpreter said, with reference to the sermon, that, as there were no sheep in that part of Ceylon, and consequently no shepherds, he was unable to explain very clearly the Bible figure of the Good Shepherd, for his hearers never saw anything of that sort. Canon Tristram asked in surprise, "How, then, did you explain what I said?" "Oh!" he replied, "I turned it into a buffalo that had lost its calf, and went into the jungle to find it." The figure of a shepherd's tenderness and love for the lambs of his flock lost its main force, with that congregation, because it was written for a very different people.

Because the Bible is written in human language it needs human helps to its understanding. Because it was written primarily by Orientals for Orientals, it needs Oriental lights for its fullest illumination. Much can be gained from it by any one who is single hearted and simple minded in its faithful study. More can be gained by one who studies it in the light of the best helps, and who, as he studies, prays the faith-filled prayer, "Lord, open thou mine eyes, that I may behold wondrous things out of thy law."

Philadelphia, Pa.

GLEANINGS FROM THE BIBLE MARGINS

GLEANINGS FROM THE BIBLE MARGINS

BY PROFESSOR JOHN H. BERNARD, D.D.

Most people possess an ordinary English Bible, with references and marginal notes, but we believe that, if the truth were known, it would be found that these notes and references are read by comparatively few. Certain it is that any one who studies them with care and diligence will gain a knowledge, not only of the meaning of the sacred writings themselves, but of the facts as to the text of Holy Scripture, which will be to him or her a valuable possession for life. We are so convinced of this that we propose to give a few samples of these notes, accessible to all, but studied by few. We are not writing for scholars, but for plain people, who love and value their Bibles. And for the present we confine ourselves to the New Testament.

And, first, let us say that the information given in the margins as to the quotations from the Old Testament to be found in the New, is of inestimable value to the student of Holy Scripture. Roughly speaking, there are something like one thousand quotations of phrases or sentences from the Jewish Bible in the Gospels, Epistles, and Revelation; and very often the full meaning of an apostolic maxim, or even of a precept of our Lord, is lost because the reference in the margin has not been looked out. Most people will admit this readily enough, but only those who have acted on the rule of verifying *all* the marginal references in their daily portion can tell how true it is. For instance, "Thou shalt love thy neighbor as thyself," which our Lord laid down as the second great commandment, is to be found in the law; namely, in Leviticus 19:18. All our Lord's answers to the tempter which he prefaced by the words "it is written," are taken, as the margin tells us, from one book of the Old Testament, and that the Book of Deuteronomy,—not the book that we should have guessed, had we not known. The "parable to them which are bidden to a feast," recommending them to take a lowly position, is practically a quotation from the Book of Proverbs.

It is interesting to note that Zaccheus's statement as to his ordinary conduct, "If I have taken anything from any man by false accusation, I restore it *fourfold,*" shows that he was accustomed to act in strict conformity with the Jewish law. Compare Exodus 22 : 1, and 2 Samuel 12 : 6. But references like this are probably not passed over so frequently as those of which we are about to speak.

Every one has noticed the careful explanations, given in the margin, of weights and measures and coins; for example, "bushel," "farthing," "penny," "talent," "pound," are all noted at the side of the text. Not all, perhaps, are explained quite satisfactorily; for instance, in Matthew 17 : 24, 27, the marginal notes in the Authorized Version do not bring out clearly—as the Revised Version does—that the "piece of money" found in the fish's mouth was a "shekel," and therefore exactly enough to defray the "tribute" for two persons, at half a shekel a head. But in general the notes are interesting, and as full as is necessary.

More significant than any of these are what may be called the *critical* notes in the Authorized Version. These are the statements in the margin which call our attention to the fact that the manuscripts vary, and that therefore the "reading" (as it is called) is not quite certain. These are more numerous than is sometimes observed, though, indeed,—it must be confessed,—they are not selected with the best possible judgment. But yet, as they bring before our minds the significant fact that the text of Holy Scripture has not come down to us absolutely pure and uncorrupted, they are worth looking at. Many of them—most of them—record a trivial difference in the original Greek manuscripts, which bears little on the sense; for example, it does not matter very much, for most of us, whether or not the words, "And Josias begat Jakim, and Jakim begat Jechonias," are an integral part of the text in Matthew 1 : 11, or not; and so we pass by, probably, without attention, the unassuming note which tells that "some read" these words.

But it is more instructive to read that verse 36 of chapter 17 of St. Luke's Gospel "is wanting in most Greek copies;" for this sets us upon asking how such a difference could arise. The answer is simple enough. In Matthew 24 : 40, Authorized Version, we find : " Then shall two be in the field ; the one shall be taken, and the other left. Two women shall be grinding at the mill ; the one shall be taken, and the other left."

Now by St. Luke only the latter of these sayings was recorded ; but when scribes began to copy the Gospels out, some of them tried to remove the apparent disagreement between the two evangelists by supplying the missing clause in the third Gospel from the parallel passage in the first. This was a common practice with scribes in early times, and many "various readings" of the sacred text are the result. In the particular case before us, although the evidence is such that scholars have concluded that the disputed words form no part of the genuine text of St. Luke, yet no doctrinal question can possibly be affected, as every one agrees that they were recorded by St. Matthew as having been spoken by the Lord.

Another case where the marginal reading is to be preferred to the reading adopted in the text of the Authorized Version, is in Ephesians 6 : 9. In this place the address of St. Paul to masters as to their duty to their servants, becomes much more forcible when we follow the margin : " And ye masters, do the same things unto them, forbearing threatening, knowing that *both your Master and theirs* is in heaven, and that there is no respect of persons with him." Again, in Acts 25 : 6, though no practical question is affected by the " reading," we get—as it seems—a clearer sense by following the margin, " When Felix had tarried among them *not more than eight or ten days*, he went down unto Cæsarea." And if we adopt the various readings alluded to in the margin of 2 Peter 2 : 18 (as the Revisers do), we shall get a far better meaning of the whole passage. It is not those who "*were clean escaped* from them who live in error," that are enticed in the lusts of the flesh, but those " who *are just escaping.*" In this case the Authorized Version, though suggesting the right reading in the margin, does not give a clear or good explanation of it there.

Other cases where the marginal note is to be preferred to the text are 1 Peter 2 : 21, and 2 Peter 2 : 2, the difference in the former case being one which often causes confusion ; namely, the difference between "we" and "you,"—two words which are much more alike in Greek than they are in English. Very often, however, the marginal reading is best left in the margin, and the text of the Authorized Version is to be preferred. Thus, in 1 Corinthians 15 : 31, "your rejoicing" is better than "our rejoicing." And in 2 Peter 2 : 11, the marginal alternative is quite unworthy of consideration, and would be extremely difficult to explain. The only reason for its insertion, even as a note, seems to be that it is adopted in the Latin translation, which forms the "Authorized Version" of the Roman Catholic Church. And in like manner the variants recorded in Matthew 26 : 26 ; Luke 10 : 22 ; Hebrews 10 : 17, and James 2 : 18, are not of sufficient authority to entitle them to displace the ordinary text. The only one of these of much interest is the last, and it probably arose through a misunderstanding of the Apostle's argument.

But the note on Acts 13 : 18 is very instructive. "About the time of forty years suffered he their manners in the wilderness," said St. Paul, speaking of God's dealings with the children of Israel. Now the marginal note tells us that there is some doubt as to which of two Greek words—very like in sound and spelling, but unlike in sense—is to be read. Some Greek manuscripts have one, and some have the other. And so it is possible—though, on the whole, not probable—that what St. Paul may have said was "about the time of forty years bare he them as a nursing father in the wilderness," with an allusion to the words of Deuteronomy 1 : 31, as generally read, "in the wilderness where thou hast seen how that the Lord thy God bare thee, as a man doth bear his son." And the marginal note farther adds that the great preacher Chrysostom, who was bishop of Constantinople about the year 400, understood the passage in the latter way, and had the corresponding reading before him.

This note is remarkable as suggesting the importance of what are called "patristic" citations of Scripture. Chrysostom, no doubt, and the men of his day, had access to manuscripts of the Bible much earlier than any that have come down to us; and so, when weighing the evidence for or against a debated "reading," it is of the utmost value to know what reading was adopted by the Christian men of the early centuries of our era.

The next note that we quote is also one in which appeal is made to a Christian writer of an age earlier than our own. This time it is not on a question of reading, but of interpretation. In Mark 7 : 3 there is a word in the Greek which has perplexed all the commentators. The Authorized Version gives "The Pharisees, and all the Jews, except they wash their hands oft, eat not." And the margin gives an alternative for "oft" which has been adopted in the Revised Version; namely, "diligently." It also tells us that the Greek word literally means "with the fist," and that the explanation of this given by Theophylact (who was archbishop of Bulgaria in the eleventh century, and a famous commentator), was that it meant "up to the elbow." Theophylact's interpretation may not be correct, but it is noted in the margin as one that must have even yet a certain authority.

In a very considerable number of verses the translations suggested in the margin have claims upon our attention superior to those of the rendering in the text, and thus they are always worthy of study. Notice how much force is added to the parable of the ten virgins when we render Matthew 25 : 8 : "Give us of your oil; for our lamps are going out." When these sad words are spoken, the lamps are not yet quite extinguished. Or again, "Whosoever hath not, from him shall be taken even that which he thinketh he hath" (Luke 8 : 18), conveys a terrible warning to self-deceivers, which the ordinary rendering does not so immediately suggest. Or take any of the numerous passages in which the verb "to offend" means to cause to offend, to cause to stumble, as the margin tells. For instance, "If thy hand offend thee, cut it off." What does that mean? But render "If thy hand cause thee to offend, cut it off," and the meaning becomes clear. In John 10 : 24 we have, in the Authorized Version, the Jews asking the Lord, "How long dost thou make us to doubt?" But that is not what they said. Turn to the margin : "How long dost thou hold us in suspense?"—a very different and a much more intelligible question.

We have taken an example from each of the Gospels. Here is one from the Acts. In St. Paul's speech to the Athenians at the Areopagus, the Authorized Version fails to make clear the point of one sentence at least. "As I passed by," he says (Acts 17 : 23), "and beheld the objects of your worship, I found an altar," etc. He alludes to the number of statues of the gods for which Athens was famous, not to the "devotions" which the Athenians were offering up in his presence. The margin here saves us from a complete misapprehension of the Apostle's words.

It would be easy to collect a number of instances similar to the above, in which there can be no reasonable doubt that the marginal translation is better than the translation in the text; but space fails, and we must be brief. Suffice it to say that the following references, if studied, will all show some point of interest: Matthew 6 : 1 ; 23 : 18 ; 24 : 33 ; 28 : 19 (comp. Acts 14 : 21); Mark 2 : 21 ; 6 : 17 ; 7 : 4 ; John 7 : 35; Acts 19 : 35; Colossians 1 : 13. In every one of the above-mentioned instances (as in many others) the Revised Version adopts the marginal rendering of our ordinary Bibles.

The notes to the Acts (of which we have already given a few) are more numerous and interesting, we think, than those on any other New Testament book. In the thirteenth chapter, contrary to the usual habit of the annotators, the Greek words are quoted in two verses (vs. 18, 34); and the chronological notes throughout are also to be observed. Thus to the allusion to Theudas's insurrection in Gamaliel's speech (Acts 5 : 36) is appended the probable date,—" in the third year before the account called A.D." And in Acts 21 : 38 the rising of "the Egyptian," for whom the chief captain mistook Paul, is dated in the margin : " This Egyptian rose A.D. 55." We do not say that these chronological notes are either complete or satisfactory, as in both cases there is some difficulty in determining the date ; but at least they indicate to the simplest reader that the allusions in both cases are to historical events of which we have other and fuller accounts.

Again, without the marginal note on

Acts 27 : 9, we doubt if the verse could be readily understood : "When much time was spent, and when sailing was now dangerous, because the fast was now already past, Paul admonished them ;" that is, the season was so far advanced that it was unsafe to take a long voyage. "The fast," says our marginal note, "was on the tenth day of the seventh month" (Lev. 23 : 27, 29). The "fast," in short, that is spoken of, is the great day of atonement, which was observed, according to the Mosaic law, on the 10th of the month Tisri, or about the time of the autumnal equinox. It was hazardous to undertake so long a sea journey after this date.

One more instance, and we have done. It is a simple one, but it illustrates well the value of the marginal notes, to which it is the object of this paper to direct attention. We read in Hebrews 4 : 8, "For if Jesus had given them rest, then would he not afterward have spoken of another day;" that is, if Joshua had given the people rest, if the rest of Canaan were indeed the rest of God, then would not he (that is, the Holy Spirit, whose warnings come to us in the Ninety-fifth Psalm) have continued after so long a time to speak of another day. But if it were not explained in the margin that "Jesus" is only the Greek form of the name "Joshua," it would be easy to misunderstand the verse, and to suppose that "he" who speaks "of another day" is the "Jesus" of the first part of the verse, instead of the divine Spirit.

If we had a similar marginal note in Acts 7 : 45, persons who are now puzzled to know the meaning of the statement that the tabernacle of witness was brought in with Jesus into the possession of the Gentiles, would understand that here too "Jesus" is "Joshua," the leader of the hosts of Israel.

If these few gleanings from the margins of an ordinary New Testament lead any one to search out that rich field of biblical knowledge for himself, they will not have been collected in vain. It is, of course, to be borne in mind that there are reference Bibles and reference Bibles. In some editions the references are very ill chosen, whereas in others not only such information as has been cited is given, but much more as well. And it is also to be remembered that the Revised Version is an indispensable instrument for arriving at the true meaning of the sacred text to the English reader who has no Greek. It is only to such a reader that these few notes are addressed; to scholars who have any knowledge of the Greek Testament they will already be familiar as household words.

Trinity College, Dublin, Ireland.

PLACE OF HELPS IN BIBLE STUDY

PLACE OF HELPS IN BIBLE STUDY

BY H. CLAY TRUMBULL, D.D.

In these days of multiplied helps to Bible study, there is the twofold danger of giving too much prominence to such helps, and of giving them too little prominence. There is on the one side the error of studying the helps to an understanding of the Bible, instead of studying the Bible by means of helps to its understanding; and, on the other side, there is the error of supposing that helps to an understanding of the Bible are uncalled for in Bible study. Both these errors are to be recognized and guarded against; for it is not easy to say which of them is the more misleading and dangerous.

It is unmistakably true that many

teachers study their lesson-helps a great deal more than they study the Bible. This fact it is that gives the ground for the widespread fear that lesson-helps stand in the way of Bible study; and that prompts the frequent calls for the abandonment of all such helps, and a return to the simple text of the Bible as the subject of lesson-study, without the aid of any outside helps whatsoever.

It is also unmistakably true that an intelligent study of the Bible without the aid of helps to its understanding is an impossibility; that both the study of the Bible itself and a knowledge of the truths of the Bible have made progress, in the church and in the community, in proportion as lesson-helps have multiplied; and that, to-day, those who are the most intelligent and the most thorough students of the Bible make free use of and value highly the largest variety of helps to its study and its understanding. This fact shows the baselessness of the frequently pressed claim that Bible study would be promoted by diminishing the number of lesson-helps available to the Bible student.

There is no department of human knowledge in which a man can study to advantage without the aid of outside helps to its understanding. A gardener who would know his business thoroughly needs to know something of botany, and something of chemistry, and something of Latin, and something of mathematics, and something of the laws of color and perspective, and something of a good many other branches of knowledge ; and all this is unattainable without helps to its acquirement. In the long run, the best gardener will be the man who most values, and who makes freest use of, good helps in the various lines of knowledge which are needful to his highest success in his special field of labor.

A school-boy cannot fairly comprehend Virgil without the help of a Latin lexicon, of an English dictionary, of a dictionary of classical antiquities, of a historical atlas, of a treatise on Latin poetry, of a good metrical translation of Virgil, and of notes and comments at obscure passages all along the course of his study in Virgil. As it is in these spheres, so it is in every other sphere of knowledge. Study without helps is an impossibility. He who studies most and to best advantage is sure to avail himself of all the helps he can find, and to be ready to make use of others as soon as he can lay hold of them.

There is certainly no less need of helps to Bible study than to any other branch of study. Indeed, the very fact that the range of Bible truth is so much greater than that of any other compendium of truth, and that the truths of the Bible are so much more important than any truths presented elsewhere, increases the need and the value of fitting helps to its understanding. Our ordinary English Bible is, in itself, a help to the understanding of the original Hebrew and Greek Testaments. The Revised Version of the two Testaments is a help to the understanding of our ordinary English Bible. Marginal references and a concordance are indispensable helps to the comparison of Scripture with Scripture.

An English dictionary is a needful help to an examination of the words employed in the English text. A Bible atlas is an important help to the localizing of the scene of any portion of the Bible narrative under immediate consideration. A Bible dictionary is an essential help in throwing light on manners and customs and rites and ceremonies referred to or involved in the statements of the Bible text. Helps are required to make clear the main facts concerning the authorship and the time and circumstances of writing, and the special aim, of the particular portion of the Bible which is being studied.

Unless one is willing to be ignorant of the results of the choicest scholarship of the ages in connection with the reverent study of the Book of books, he must have helps to an acquaintance with those results. If he would have the gain of the best thought of the best thinkers of all time as prompted by the truths of the passage he is examining, he will have to avail himself of helps in that direction also. In short, the more desirous one is of thoroughness and accuracy in his Bible study, the more helps to such study he will make available in the course of that study.

As a matter of fact, it is ordinarily the man who knows little or nothing about Bible study who would think of attempting to study the Bible without helps. Now and then a parent or a preacher, who remembers the time when he memorized the Bible words as a Sunday-school exercise, without any helps to an understanding of their meaning, looks with dismay, or distrust, on the multiplied helps which are put within reach of the children of to-day; and he is afraid that lesson-helps are standing in the way of Bible study. Yet if that man could bring into immediate comparison the best results of the Bible study of then, and of the Bible study of now, in the average Sunday-school, he would find that both in a general and in a particular knowledge of the Bible the Sunday-school pupil of to-day is far in advance of the Sunday-school pupil of a generation ago.

The multiplication of helps to Bible study has resulted in an increase of intelligent Bible study. Even though lesson-helps are too often studied by themselves, instead of being made helps to Bible study, no Bible student can have too many such helps for wise use in his study, any more than a student in any other realm of research can have too large a library to select from in the course of his special studies.

But how can a man be sure that he is using lesson-helps as an aid to Bible study, instead of studying the lesson-helps themselves, when he ought to be studying the Bible? That is the practical question; and it is a question that can be answered with comparative ease. From the beginning to the close of the study of a Bible lesson, it should be the Bible text itself that is the object and center of study. Whether the student has a library of separate volumes available to him, or is making use of a compend of lesson-helps in some single volume, or in some periodical, he ought first to look at the Bible text rather than at the notes or comments which are designed to make it clear. And from that time onward he should study the text with the help of the helps, rather than the helps in the light of the text.

In examining the particular Bible text of his lesson, a teacher may need to consider who wrote it ; and when, and where, and to whom, and under what circumstances, and why, it was written ; and what is the context of this passage. This knowledge would, perhaps, have to be obtained at the start, and therefore to be looked up forthwith by means of some available lesson-help. In the light of this knowledge the text should be examined anew.

The words of the text ought to be weighed carefully in the sense in which they are employed just here. As a help to their understanding, trustworthy critical notes can be consulted by the ordinary Bible student who is not an independent Hebrew or Greek scholar ; but constantly the student should turn back from the help to the text, using the help only in order to make clearer the text. The meaning of the text as a whole ought to be sought in itself as it stands, rather than in the comments on it which are available to the student; but when a student has gained his own idea of the meaning of the text, he can wisely turn to the writings of others in order to ascertain whether the meaning he sees in the text is a correct one.

So, again, as to the thought and applications of that text, the student ought first to seek them for himself in the text, and then test or correct them, or add to them, by means of the best helps which are secured to him. The text should be the center of his study and of his interest. The helps should be looked at and made use of only as helps to an understanding of that text. They are not to be counted as of value in themselves, nor are they to be studied by themselves.

To suppose that the Bible can be sufficiently studied without the aid of any human helps to its understanding, is to presuppose the inspiration of the student of the Bible, rather than of its writers. To suppose that the best helps to Bible study in the world can be compared with the Bible text itself, is to presuppose the inspiration of the commentators rather than of the Bible writers. Neither commentators as commentators, nor Bible students as Bible students, can be counted as a specially inspired class, whatever help they may have had from God in their work.

It is for each Bible student to use helps in his study as helps to his study, not as substitutes for his study. He is to use his helps in such a manner as shall enable him to study more and to better advantage than he could without them, not to enable him to get on with less study or effort than if he had no helps in his study.

The place of helps in Bible study is that of an auxiliary aid to the understanding of the text itself, as that text is studied under the guidance of the Holy Spirit who inspired it, and who can make its teachings clear to him who studies it reverently, with the assistance of all available helps, in dependence on the Holy Spirit's guidance.

Philadelphia, Pa.

HOW TO USE BIBLE
COMMENTARIES

HOW TO USE BIBLE COMMEN-
TARIES

BY THE RIGHT REV. C. J. ELLICOTT, D.D.
BISHOP OF GLOUCESTER AND BRISTOL

There is, perhaps, no practical subject connected with the intelligent study of Holy Scripture of more real importance at the present time than that which is specified in the heading of this article. By the great blessing of Almighty God, an awakened interest in his Holy Word is everywhere showing itself.

Not only are our intelligent laity now manifesting a real desire to arrive truly at the full meaning of the message which God's Word has for them in these closing years of an eventful century, but they are increasingly desirous, so far as they can properly do so, to assist in bringing that knowledge home to the younger members of the flock of Christ, in Sunday-schools, Bible teachings, and other agencies for making the saving Word more widely known. To such,—and it is to such and for such that we are writing this paper,—it is of the utmost importance to be guided generally in the choice of commentaries, and especially in the best and most profitable use of them.

This knowledge it is the object of this article to supply in a broad and general manner, and in such form as may help not only to the better use of commentaries, but to such a use as may most facilitate the intelligent explanation of God's Word to others. We must not only be careful in our selection of commentaries, and wise in our use of them, but we must so assimilate the knowledge they give us that we can use it with ease and with freedom to others.

This is the great purpose to be aimed at, especially by those for whom this article is more particularly intended, and it is the purpose which shall be clearly kept sight of in the advice I shall venture to give. Still I can only do so in a broad and general manner. My knowledge of the commentaries in use among those to whom I have the happiness and responsibility of writing is very limited, and my acquaintance with the extent to which they may be used more limited still. My comments must then be on the subject generally, rather than on any particular exemplifications of it. Still, there are three or four broad groups into which nearly all commentaries may be separated, and on these it will be conducive to clearness to make a few preliminary remarks.

Our commentaries, for the most part, have one or other of these three elements mainly predominant,—the historical, the exegetical, or the suggestive and deductive.

In the commentaries of the class first named, the object of the writer is to bring before the reader all that knowledge of time, place, and circumstances, which puts the reader on a kind of level with those who first heard or received the message, and makes the outward meaning of that message the more felt and appreciated.

In commentaries of the second group, the object on the part of the writer is to bring the fuller and inner meaning of the inspired words before the mind of the reader, to set forth the sequence of thought and the logical connection, and to clear up any apparent obscurity that there might be in the words of the sacred text, whether as they appear in their original forms or as they are represented in their translated dress. Such commentaries we commonly speak of as exegetical or interpretative. They form by far the largest class of the commentaries with which ordinary readers come in contact.

Nevertheless, we must not forget the third group,—unfortunately a very limited one,—in which the predominant desire of the writer is to help his more thoughtful readers to draw those inferences, whether doctrinal or practical, which flow from the words of the sacred author, but which may not by any means be obvious to the general reader. Of this class, the well-known Gnomon of Bengel is an eminent example, the force and life of which has, to a larger extent than we might have supposed, been preserved in the recent English translation. To really benefit, however, by this remarkable and almost unique commentary, we must go to the terse language in which it was originally written.

These are the three groups into which, sufficiently for our present purposes, we may roughly consider commentaries to be divided. Let us now consider how best to make use of them.

The first plain rule to follow is this: to define to ourselves quite clearly *the purpose and object* of our seeking the aid of the commentator. Is it that we may be helped in our devotional reading of Holy Scripture? or is it that we may acquire generally, as students, a more full and accurate knowledge of it? or is it that we may obtain such a knowledge as will, probably, be most helpful to others to whom we may desire to impart it? or, in other words, are we proposing to read God's Word more especially for the support of the soul and the development of our inward life, or for the illumination of the mind, or to give helpful instruction to others? When we have clearly defined to ourselves the leading aspects of the purpose of our study, we shall at once find ourselves able, not only more wisely to choose and use the commentary, but to read with far more benefit to the soul the blessed Book itself.

I am persuaded that many, and those, too, godly and sincere persons, often read their Bible in a very vague way, and with a very undefined purpose. They regard Bible reading as a kind of religious exercise, good and edifying in the very fact of being done, but not as either one or other of the two things which it ought to be,—either a giving of light to the mind, or a bringing of life to the soul. Hence it is, that, as a natural consequence, the commentary, even if of a general character, and more or less useful for either purpose, is rarely studied in any really profitable manner. There is no definite purpose in reading the text, and so no thoughtful assimilation of the more instructive portions of the commentary. Both are read together without any settled scope ; both become mixed up together in the thoughts ; and both, I fear, are very soon forgotten.

Our first duty, then, is to make quite clear to ourselves our purpose in approaching God's Word. When that is made clear, the choice of a commentary becomes much more easy. Let us suppose that it be for the edification of the soul, and for what might be called a distinctly devotional purpose. In such a case, we should naturally choose a commentary of a *suggestive* character ; a commentary which made its chief object the drawing forth from the inspired words of the deeper teaching which they involved, whether in the form of the full significance of the recorded event, or in the deduction that could be safely and certainly drawn from the exhortation or the teaching.

Often will the meditative reader find a complete vista of mysterious thought opened out to him by a true meditative exposition of even the simplest and most familiar passages; often questions of the deepest spiritual interest, present and future, unexpectedly disclose themselves, and, even if they are such as to admit no certain answer from our present knowledge, awaken fruitful thoughts and meditations which quicken and elevate the soul, and enlarge all its hopes and sympathies.

Take, for example, such a well-known and familiar text as the third beatitude, "Blessed are the meek, for they shall inherit the earth" (Matt. 5 : 5). "The earth." What earth? When? How? Is this only a solemn recital of a few familiar words of the Psalmist (Psa. 27 : 11), with no further reference than is to be attributed to the passage in the Old Testament? Is it only, as such a commentator as Meyer suggests, a Christian sublimation of it, and a reference to the Messianic Kingdom? Or is there, above and besides this, a mystic reference to some blessed and as yet undisclosed future; and is Bengel right, or otherwise, when he directs the attention of the spiritual reader to such a parallel as Revelation 5 : 10? Such instances could be indefinitely multiplied; and it is for the unfolding of such that what we have termed the *suggestive* commentary is especially needed, and better calculated than any other to quicken the spiritual life of the devout reader, and to show to him, even if it cannot fully explain them, the soul-stirring mysteries of the inspired Word.

If the purpose be rather for the acquiring of a knowledge of the general meaning of Holy Scripture, and for the understanding the current of the reasoning, or the pertinence of the allusions, if, in a word, the reader places himself rather in the study than in his closet, then, clearly, a more general commentary is desirable.

And, thanks be to God, there is no dearth of these both in America and in England. Our common mother-tongue has been, especially of late, more successfully employed in the setting forth of the truth as it is found in the Holy Scriptures, than any other language on the earth, the German not excepted. The general reader who seeks will easily and readily find.

If, again, the purpose of studying God's Word be more especially for the acquisition of such a knowledge of it as could readily and profitably be imparted to others,—to the class or the Sunday-school,—then those commentaries should be sought out in which the *historical* element is more distinctly prominent, and in which illustration, rather than doctrinal teaching or evolution of the thought of the sacred writer, more generally predominates. In teaching others, especially the younger members of the flock of Christ, what we most need is that knowledge which helps to bring the whole scene if it be narrative, or the whole circumstances if it be exhortation, to the minds of those to whom the instruction is to be given. The mere interpretation of the passage takes but little hold on the younger mind; the application is soon forgotten; but the circumstances, the surroundings, the history, and the illustrative elucidation, are all eagerly listened to, and rapidly and profitably assimilated,— perhaps never to be completely forgotten.

But we have now dwelt sufficiently on our first rule, though certainly not more than its importance requires. It may be briefly summed up in this short sentence: Make clear to the mind the leading purpose for which Holy Scripture is read, and choose the commentary accordingly. This is the first rule, and the chief rule. The two remaining rules, which we will briefly specify, are more to be considered rules of detail, but still each of some practical importance.

Of these two rules, the first relates to the time at which the commentary should be used; the second, to that form of commentary which should take the precedence of every other.

The first of these two points is really of great importance. Nearly always, even by more thoughtful students, the sacred text and the commentary are read contemporaneously. The text and commentary are commonly on the same page, and the eye glances from the one to the other, the mind scarcely being able to realize whether or not it has met with any actual difficulty in the text. The consequence is, that the mental hold on the passage is very weak. Its presumed meaning has been arrived at far too easily for any durable impression to have been made. It soon fades from memory, and leaves no trace either on the intellectual or devotional side of the mind of the reader. There may be just a hazy knowledge of the passage, but not that spiritual understanding which is absolutely necessary, not merely for the teacher, but for the sober thinker, who is faithfully searching for the sake of finding the true significance of the written Word, in reference to daily life and practice. The error has been, that the text has not been read, *and carefully thought over, before* any reference to the commentary. It is that thinking over what has been read that really imprints the passage upon the memory and upon the soul. The difficulties are realized; their solution may not be perceived; but the very fact that it is so makes that solution, when arrived at by a reference to the commentary, tenaciously remembered.

Our rule then to the earnest student is,

—on no account refer to the commentary until the passage, as it stands in the inspired text, has been fully thought out, as far as the mental power of the reader enables him to do it. Try even, further, to deduce from it the deeper considerations which it appears to involve. Then, with the mind thus prepared, quickened, and made conscious of what it needs for a complete understanding of the text, go to the commentary. If it satisfies the mind, rest content, and assimilate what it teaches. If not, reserve the point on which the mind is still unsatisfied, for further, and, it may be, for better aid. In this way a true and exact knowledge of Scripture will be steadily acquired, and commentaries put to their right use,—that of helping earnest effort, not of abbreviating or superseding it.

Our third and last rule is,—before any other commentary is used, use the Holy Scriptures themselves as a commentary, by means of well-chosen parallel passages. This, again, is a rule of the utmost moment. By following it, not only will the first, best, and surest explanation of the passage under consideration have been secured, but also a knowledge of Holy Scripture generally, and of its blessed harmonies, be silently acquired, more surely and more abidingly than in any other way that could be named.

Such, then, are the rules we venture to give; such, what we deem to be the best use of commentaries. If followed only for a short time, their value will, we are persuaded, become almost self-evident, and their benefit to the student fully recognized. They are simple, but they are true and tested rules; and, as such, we commend them to our readers.

The Palace, Gloucester, England.

RIGHT SPIRIT IN OLD TESTAMENT STUDY

RIGHT SPIRIT IN OLD TESTAMENT STUDY

BY PROFESSOR WILLIS J. BEECHER, D.D.

Actually, I intend to discuss only a single specification under this generic subject; but the statement of the subject in its generic form serves me instead of an introduction. He who studies the Old Testament with a right spirit will think it worth his while to try to understand the Old Testament correctly. In particular, if one regards the Old Testament as the inspired word of God, he should be confident that what God says has a meaning, that God knew what it was best to say, and that he who aims to find out just what God has said in the Scriptures is the one who most honors the Scriptures.

Unfortunately, this is not a superfluous thing to say. We have all formed certain habits, due in part to our very reverence for the Word of God, which operate to prevent our thorough mastery of its contents.

First, we go to the Bible to be fed by it. This is commendable. This is what the Bible is for. But in doing this, we often study a passage simply for the so-called practical points it contains. We even import practical points into a passage, connecting them with it by analogies, or even by mere fancies. A good deal of our most telling study of the Bible is of this sort. I think that devout persons will never cease from this mode of study. No doubt, through study of this kind, the Holy Spirit feeds them from the Word. We may even concede that this is the best available form of study for some persons, in some circumstances.

But this form of study, if exclusively practiced, diverts us from a thorough study for the complete meaning of the passage. It leads us to feel satisfied when we have gained three or four superficial points, while we leave the rest of the meaning unexplored. It leads us to give our attention to some spiritual truth incidentally connected with the passage, to the entire neglect of the central meanings of the passage itself. There are men and women of gifts and of power who never study the Bible in any other way than this. They have accumulated a few dozen points. Whenever they study any chapter of the Bible, no matter what, their study consists in finding some of these points there; and they find nothing else.

I am not speaking of those who pervert the Word of God, nor of those who are careless and superficial in their use of it, but of the mistaken methods of some who study it reverently and profitably. Suppose we take pains to avoid this mistaken method. Suppose that, instead of hunting for points, we hunt, first of all, for the proper meaning conveyed by the words and sentences used, and for the whole of that meaning.

When the Old Testament records historical transactions, suppose we try to find out exactly what those transactions were. When it sketches human conduct for us, suppose we attempt to form an intelligible idea of the conduct so sketched. When it draws word pictures, or uses figures of speech, suppose we take pains to look at the pictures, and open our imagination to the figures. Suppose we let the practical points go until we have a reasonably distinct idea of the meaning of the passage. Surely God knows what truths we most need to learn from revelation. Suppose we so far defer to his judgment as simply to learn the lesson he has set for us, in the form in which he has set it, instead of picking out such bits of it as we imagine are best suited to our needs. If we really master the meaning of any part of revelation, we may be certain that the practical lessons that will follow such a mastery are those that are best worth learning.

Again, it is blessedly true that the Bible is a book for little children. But one result of this is that most of us learned the contents of the Old Testament narratives when we were babies. We think we have understood them ever since we were babies. We are confirmed in this by comparing our ideas of them with those of other people who also learned them when they were babies. And this goes on for generation after generation. In this way there has been established a thoroughly infantile traditional interpretation of much of the Old Testament narrative.

As a matter of fact, a great deal of so-called study of the Old Testament consists less in an examination of what the Old Testament says than in the handing down of nursery traditions as to what the Old Testament means. And the differences between what the Old Testament actually says and our current notions of what it says are sometimes startling. A due respect to the Bible and its divine Author requires that we should test our notions as to its contents by a careful study of those contents themselves. That is just what most of us are in danger of not doing. Instead of doing it, we are apt to assume that we know all that it is worth while to know in regard to the narratives, and that nothing further is requisite except to make good points from what we know.

If any of us have become dissatisfied with our crude and childish knowledge of Old Testament matters, and are seeking to replace this by a more intelligent and mature knowledge, we want, first of all, to study carefully the text of the Old Testament. If we cannot read it in Hebrew, we can at least use the Revised English version, and thus get several degrees nearer to the original than the old version would bring us.

Then we need to form the habit of examining all the evidence that is within our reach in regard to each transaction. If we can do no more, we can at least attempt to examine all that the Bible says in regard to the transaction, and can do this in the light of the known facts of biblical geography.

Further, we need to remember that the Bible narratives are not history in the sense of purporting to be a complete account of the events recorded, written mainly for the purpose of perpetuating a knowledge of the events. They are selections from history, written for purposes of religious teaching. It does not follow that they are historically untrustworthy, but it follows that one who persists in regarding them as complete accounts of all that happened in certain cases will be led to interpret them erroneously.

One who is really trying to understand the contents of the Old Testament must study those contents continuously. It will not answer his purpose to pick out a dozen verses in every third chapter, and study those verses. He cannot in that way understand the selected verses, much less the writing of which they are a part.

The International Lessons are generally so selected that it is possible, in connection with them, to make a continuous study of the books of the Bible. "Continuous study" classes ought to be formed in every Sunday-school. It would be no very severe task for a mature person to read three or four consecutive chapters a week with sufficient care so that he can state from memory their most important contents, and follow the events on a map. No extraordinary mental strain would be involved in keeping this up by advance and review work from week to week for six months. But the doing of this would be for many a long step forward in knowledge of the Bible.

In studying the first six books of the Old Testament, we cannot altogether ignore the current critical controversies. On this point, it is exceedingly important that we pursue a correct method, and two or three hints will be of value. First, no one disputes that these six books, in their present form, existed in the time of Christ, and were recognized alike by him, his disciples, and his opponents, as a part of the Scriptures. Hence we have a right to study them, just as they are, as having scriptural authority. This right does not depend on the adjustment of any disputed questions. For most purposes of Sunday-school instruction it is as well to let these questions entirely alone.

Second, the first step toward an intelligent study of these questions is a reasonably thorough mastery of the contents of the books as they stand. In this matter, the contents of the books furnish almost the only data we have to reason from, and one is not qualified to enter upon the argument until he understands the premises. Under this rule, we ought to have been spared a large part of all that has been published on these questions. Under this rule only a small percentage of the members of our Sunday-schools are qualified to enter upon studies of this kind, though this small percentage includes in all many tens of thousands of persons.

Third, a fair-minded man, if he undertakes to reach conclusions here, will take the trouble to understand the questions involved, and to distinguish one question from another. It is supposable that either party to a controversy may be correct in some of its propositions and incorrect in others. The person who simply lumps all the questions together, and then takes sides with one party or the other, pursues a course that is lazy and unjust, and is deadening to his own mental and spiritual perceptions.

To make this clear, I must briefly state my own opinion on some of the points of difference between what we may call the "old view," and what we may call the "new view" in Pentateuchal criticism. I think that those who hold the new view are evidently correct when they insist that the proper literary unit here is the Hexateuch, and not the Pentateuch. I think they are clearly correct when they affirm that the six books bear marks of having been made, like the books of Kings and Chronicles, by the process of putting together writings that previously existed. I think they are correct in some of their more general classifications of the materials.

When they go beyond this, and attempt a minute analysis, I think they are taking positions which, in the nature of the case, cannot be proved, though some of them cannot be disproved. When their opponents affirm that Moses wrote the whole Pentateuch, and that to doubt this is to discredit the sacred Word of God, and then afterward admit the existence of post-Mosaic elements in some dozens of passages, and explain these as annotations made by unknown persons at unknown dates, at some time during the thousand years between Phinehas and Ezra, I think that their reasoning is simply suicidal.

When the men of the new view affirm

that the several parts of the Hexateuch were written at different periods, but all some hundreds of years later than Moses, I think that their proposition is contradicted by the evidence in the case. When the verdict is in, I think it will be that the legislation of the Hexateuch is genuinely Mosaic, and that the whole Hexateuch is in such a sense due to Moses and Joshua—to writing done by them, to writing done by others under their supervision, to literary impulses originating with them—as to justify the assertion that they are properly the authors of the six books. I hold, further, that in the processes by which the Hexateuch was produced there was an element of providential guidance, and an element of miraculous inspiration, constituting the complete work a part of the inspired word of God.

I have thus stated my opinions, not for the purpose of advocating them, but to illustrate the fact that several entirely different questions are involved in the current controversies, that some of these questions are separable from others, and that therefore one does injustice to his own intellect and conscience if he simply blocks them all together, and, on the one side or the other, raises the cry of "heretic," or "moss-back," as the case may be.

For those who wish to study for themselves the analysis of Genesis, as given by the advocates of the new view, two important books have been published in recent years: "Genesis Printed in Colors," by the Rev. Dr. E. C. Bissell, of Chicago; and "Genesis of Genesis," by Professor B. W. Bacon of Yale University. Professor Bacon believes in the analysis, and Dr. Bissell does not. Dr. Bissell's book is the more compact and usable, while Professor Bacon's is more full and complete. By the use of either a reader of the English Bible can, without an extravagant outlay of time, obtain a pretty good idea of the views of the analytical critics.

Apart from all current controverted questions, he who wishes to understand the meaning of the Old Testament must pay some attention to the literary characteristics of the writings. To ignore these is to ignore a part of the revelation that God has given. For example, the Revised Version prints six passages in Genesis in separated lines as poetical. Several other passages should be so printed. Does any one doubt that the writer of Genesis found these poetical fragments already in existence, and incorporated them into his record? If any one fails to recognize them as quoted bits of poetry, can he really understand the passages? And what is true of these is true of the other literary phenomena.

Finally, if we are seeking to understand the true meaning of the Old Testament, we must come to the study with teachable spirit, imploring and obtaining the help of the divine Spirit, and ready to accept at his hands the truth, whatever it may be.

Auburn Theological Seminary.

HOW TO GET A KNOWLEDGE OF THE WHOLE NEW TESTAMENT

HOW TO GET A KNOWLEDGE OF THE WHOLE NEW TESTAMENT

BY PROFESSOR GEORGE B. STEVENS, PH.D., D.D.

There are certainly a great many intelligent and earnest Christians who have long been students of the Bible, and who still feel that they have not as much real knowledge and appreciation of it as the labor expended ought to have given them. Many parts of it—even some of the most important parts of the New Testament—are still obscure and enigmatical to them.

To suppose a case chosen almost at random : Ask the most intelligent Christians in any average congregation to give an account of the Epistle to the Colossians, what ideas it contains, what it was written for, etc., how many could render any intelligible answer? Or, suppose the book were handed them, and they were asked what Paul had in mind in speaking of "philosophy," "a voluntary humility and worshiping of angels," "holding fast the Head," "wisdom in will-worship," and numerous other terms. If answers should be slow and difficult, it would be no wonder; for the appreciation of these terms and of the letter as a whole requires a good deal of information about the Colossian Church, the errors of the time, and the whole situation which called out the Epistle.

But this is precisely the sort of information which is indispensable for the understanding of the biblical books. They are largely blind books when their occasion, situation, and purpose are not understood. We wish to urge the importance of acquiring such knowledge, and to show how it can be done.

Let us keep by our illustration,—Colossians. We said that a good deal of historic information about the book is necessary in order to understand it. Yes; but a great deal of such knowledge can be gained in a very short time when once it has been carefully accumulated, condensed, and presented in attractive form by competent scholars. It would be possible to read in thirty minutes a succinct statement of the occasion and aim of the Colossian Epistle which should embody the essential results of investigation on the subject, and which would give to that noble letter a wholly new interest and a far clearer meaning.

Many seem to think that the Bible can be understood by studying the Bible alone. Its practical teachings may be so gained, of course; but in any proper sense it cannot be so understood. All the aids of historic investigation must be employed to help us to place ourselves in the situation in which the books were composed, so that we can appreciate the special aim of the book, and may see the meaning of the peculiar terms which the author employs in order to attain his purpose. We are confident that this is the kind of information which is more needed than any other in order to open the meaning of the biblical books, particularly the Epistles, and to make them stand out in their true individuality and power.

Limiting our view to the New Testament, let us consider how it is practicable for one to gain such a knowledge of each book of the New Testament as a whole as will throw this new light upon the language, the allusions, and the various arguments which find place in it.

Let one take in hand some readable yet reliable manual on New Testament introduction, such as Farrar's "Messages of the Books," Lumby's or Dods's "Introduction to the New Testament." It were better to have and use more than one of these. The student should not, we think, begin with the Gospels,—partly because they are practically better understood by almost all Christians than the rest of the New Testament, and partly because the critical questions connected with them are so intricate and difficult.

He will do best to commence with the Epistles of St. Paul. He will soon ascertain from his manual in what order they were written, how they are to be grouped, and to what part of the apostle's life each group belongs. He will thus learn the leading characteristics of each group. Then let him set himself to learn from his handbooks, and by reading up the New Testament references which he will find, as much as possible about the historic situation of the first group, 1 and 2 Thessalonians. He will study the story of the founding of the Thessalonian Church in Acts, and will find out what was Paul's experience there; he will ascertain what circumstances called out each letter, and what was the relation of the two to each other.

At every step in this work the passages which are referred to in the manual should be carefully examined. It will take no long time to learn the condition of the Thessalonian congregation and the peculiar troubles there which called out the Epistles. Then they may be read as a whole with entirely new appreciation; and the knottiest passages, which, in advance of the knowledge of the situation meant little or nothing to the reader, will be found to be of chief interest, and to constitute the most important parts of the apostle's whole course of thought.

In a study like this the use of the right sort of books is all-important. If one takes too technical or too dull a book as a guide to introduction, he is almost sure to grow discouraged before he has really worked himself into the subject, and so to give it up altogether. Farrar's book is a good one with which to begin, because it is graphic and popular in style; then the short but pithy chapters of Dr. Dods's volume would be the better appreciated.

If then the student have time and inclination, the period of the apostle's life whose meaning has been thus far opened can be made matter of more extended reading in such books as Sabatier's "The Apostle Paul," which has recently appeared in English, or Farrar's "Life of St. Paul," in which the place of his Epistles in the apostle's career is so fully set forth.

But we have made only a beginning. True, but that is a great thing if we have made an intelligent beginning, and have learned how to read two of the Pauline Epistles, even though they be the easiest of them all. That is more than thousands of people can do who have read the Bible all their life. We must go forward. Our next group comprises Galatians, 1 and 2 Corinthians, and Romans. Here again we must get some general information about the group as a whole, so as to understand the issues which called out these greatest efforts of the apostle's mind. Then let them be taken up one by one.

Learn what is available of the churches to which they were written, the peculiarities of the people composing them, their special faults or dangers, and thus find out to what sort of a case the Epistle in question was adapted. As individual passages are looked up which illustrate one or another point, a new light will begin to shine into the whole book until it stands out clear cut in the mind, where it will have forever after an individuality and character of its own.

This is the only way in which the Epistles

can be marked off from each other so that each will stand for something distinctive. Commonly they are all in a jumble. But they have as great differences of tone, content, style, and diction, as the letters of any person nowadays would have which should be addressed to persons in different places, under the most various conditions, and in widely removed periods of time. Even though the general subject of all the letters in such a case were religion, we should expect great differences of method and matter. This we have in the case of St. Paul's Epistles.

And so the work must go on from point to point in the same method. Does it seem a hopelessly long task? It is not. There are but twenty-seven books in the New Testament. We are speaking now to those who do already take some time to study (or read) the Bible. It takes no more time to study it intelligently and in a way adapted to yield definite knowledge, than to study it haphazard. It takes less time, in fact. Will it be a very difficult study? No. Many difficult questions will, of course, be met with,—many points on which the best scholars cannot agree. Leave them to the specialists. The most essential things can be ascertained for certain. Make sure of *them.*

Will it be a dry and tedious study? No, provided one be interested in studying the Bible at all. It will make all previous Bible study which was carried on piecemeal and without any method seem tame enough, and will show the student that he has never before known what real interest in Bible study was.

Why should it be thought impracticable for every intelligent Christian who has an ordinary amount of time at his command to get a good knowledge of the whole New Testament? The Old Testament is an immense and difficult field, and ignorance of it is more excusable. Individual books of the New Testament, like Revelation, and individual passages in other books, are obscure and of uncertain meaning; but these may be left out of account for the purpose under discussion.

An appreciative knowledge is perfectly practicable, if it is really desired and sought with intelligent determination. The leisure of most people for a single winter would be ample for its attainment; we do not mean for a critical or minute knowledge, but for a knowledge that would include all the main facts regarding all the New Testament books,—the facts without possession of which it is absolutely impossible to read most of the books with appreciation.

The gain of such a knowledge would be incalculable. It would make reverence for the Bible intelligent and real where often it is only blind and traditional; and would really open the world of biblical truth, and make it the mind's inalienable possession.

Yale University.

HINTS ON THE STUDY OF THE GOSPELS

HINTS ON THE STUDY OF THE GOSPELS

BY PROFESSOR M. B. RIDDLE, D.D., LL.D.

The first "hint" is one "as broad as a barn-door," to quote an old saying. To study the Gospels aright, one must learn how to study. This does not imply that these narratives cannot be used with great profit by one who does not know how to study. But this article is to be about that particular use of the Gospels called "study."

This use is to be distinguished from getting a lesson, which, as a rule, consists in committing answers to certain formulated or anticipated questions; and also from reading, which is rather a passive listening to what is written than an active inquiry concerning its full significance. Nor is study identical with reflection, though the former is not complete unless it includes the latter.

This "learning how" is of far more importance than a knowledge of the best "helps," about which most make the first inquiry. For one who cannot use books aright, there are no good helps. To feel this is the first step in learning how to study the Gospels, as in all other branches of intellectual activity. Our educational methods are too often faulty in this respect, that they fail to train pupils in the use of books as tools.

The next hint is: Make for yourself a working outline of the gospel history. This is of great importance for various reasons. The Gospels are historical books, hence they ought to be studied as such. Four in number, they do not cover exactly the same periods of our Lord's life. An outline of the history is necessary to fit the narratives into each other, and each one can be better understood in consequence. A knowledge of the historical relations is indispensable, if we would understand the progress of doctrine, the method of instruction, the training of the Twelve, the significance of the miracles, and, above all, the main purpose of our Lord's work. The true perspective is historical, and only when this is recognized do we discover where the emphasis is placed in the entire narrative.

Many teachers, aware of the necessity of such knowledge, fail to set about acquiring it in the right way. They read voluminous lives of Christ, depend on harmonies and tables of chronology made for them. The time spent in constantly referring to these would be better spent in making for one's self a historical outline.

This is not so difficult as it seems. Let the attention be directed to the salient points; fix the number of Passovers first. If this vexed question cannot be settled, take one view as a working plan, and adjust the table to that view. Then, with the Gospel of Mark as the general guide, on the periods it covers, arrange the leading events by years, carefully noting the place of each Passover in the Gospel which is specially studied. One danger will be from attempting to decide all the doubtful points before constructing the outline. But do as civil engineers do: make a general survey first, the details can be arranged afterwards. When I began to write commentaries on the Gospels, I found that this method was indispensable for me in my work. After many years, I feel more and more disposed to recommend it to my pupils and to all students of the Gospels.

The next hint is: Keep in mind both the purpose of the particular Gospel you are studying, and the literary and other peculiarities of the human author. It is scarcely necessary to show the importance of this. Nor is there any difficulty in discovering how it can be done. Practically, however, too much emphasis is often laid upon the purpose of the Gospel, because it is so easy to generalize about this. Too little attention is paid to the peculiarities of the evangelists, since this involves minute, careful, and discriminating study.

The fourth hint concerns the method of dealing with particular passages, and the suggestions hold good in all biblical study. The first thing to be attempted is to master for yourself the meaning of the passage, using helps only as helping you to perceive that meaning. To be more explicit, try to understand just what the words of the passage mean, taken by themselves; then look at parallel passages and references; after that, if necessary, consult your Bible dictionary; then take the commentary you have found most trustworthy, and see how nearly right you are. If that were done thoroughly for a few months, the results would be as surprising as they would be advantageous.

Beware of using a commentary in such a way as to hinder study and discourage reflection. Having made several commentaries, and found my pupils too ready to substitute my work for their own, I say this with emphasis. Of course, no disrespect is intended to the commentator. But most people trust these helps too much.

Especially hurtful to real study is the habit of jumping to the practical lessons of a passage, as given in some "help," without carefully considering and comprehending the facts and statements of Scripture on which these lessons are based. Some good people think it a mark of great spirituality in them that they are thus eager for the spiritual truth, as they say. They are apt to be impatient with those who seek accurate explanations of the passage itself, as part of a historical narrative. But such people are wrong. God would not have revealed himself in act and fact, as he has done in Jesus Christ, if he did not intend us to study the facts of the Gospels as accurately, as scientifically, we may say, as we do the facts in nature.

This method of ignoring the historical truth for the sake of the spiritual truth (as is claimed), is doubly injurious. It injures the mind by encouraging slovenly habits of thought. It injures the heart by diminishing the power of deducing lessons for ourselves from the facts of the Gospel. It is equally, perhaps more, improper, to be so curious about grammatical, typographical, and archæological points, as to ignore the spiritual lessons. But here, as usual, there are two wrong ways to be avoided. The one right way is: accurate study of the passage as history in order to learn the spiritual lessons properly deducible from it.

The last hint is this: In studying the Gospels, keep constantly in mind the true view of the person of Christ. It is assumed that every Sunday-school teacher has settled the question for himself or herself: "What think ye of the Christ? Whose son is he?" On this question there has been theoretical unanimity for many centuries. The small fractions of nominal Christendom that dissent from the generally accepted view, have soon neglected Christ and the Gospels that tell of him. Since these narratives are about him, it is natural to assume that one cannot appreciate them, or study them profitably, unless there is a correct view taken of this person. Experience, as recorded in church history, proves that we may safely thus assume.

Heathen or half-heathen unbelievers may be asked to study the Gospels without theological bias, in order that they may draw from them the correct view of Christ. But Sunday-school teachers cannot teach much if they are not clear as to the person of Christ. Nor can they study correctly without a correct view of that person. I say "person of Christ" rather than "divinity of Christ;" for the Gospels present Jesus as the Son of Mary, a real man, and as a man rising from the dead and ascending to the right hand of God. Thus is given the crowning proof that he is the God-man, now in heaven. Believing that, keeping that constantly in mind, we have the proper stimulus to study. Feeling that he was and is a real man, we are moved to mark carefully what he said and did on earth, as a matter of history ; knowing him as the Son of God, we seek carefully the spiritual lessons in that history. Assured that he is our present Saviour, now at the right hand of God, we look for the beatings of that same human heart in the story of his life on earth, that we may feel how warmly it still beats for us.

Failing to recognize his humanity, we may neglect his human history; failing to admit his divinity, we may lose sight of the spiritual lessons of that life on earth, descending first to a purely literary study of the Gospels, and then to a neglect of them. The history of interpretation and of doctrine attests the truth of the above positions. Only when we accept Jesus Christ as the God-man, now in heaven, yet once on the earth, can we study the Gospels aright. They are designed to reveal this person; and the divine significance is indissolubly united with the human history, even as the divine and the human are united in Christ.

Western Theological Seminary.

HINTS ON THE STUDY OF THE EPISTLES

HINTS ON THE STUDY OF THE EPISTLES

BY PROFESSOR J. M. STIFLER, D.D.

The religious condition of the time in which any Epistle was written must be considered, and, as far as possible, learned. The Book of Acts is in large measure the proper introduction to the study of the Epistles.

They were written to the churches founded in Judea and in the Roman world, or to individuals connected with these churches. Churches were formed first in Judea, and then westward through Asia Minor and into Europe as far as to Rome. The Book of Acts gives the history of the spread of the gospel, and its story is easily understood.

The first thing to observe is that the apostolic churches were of two kinds: pure Jewish churches, and mixed, or Gentile, churches. They were alike in their faith that Jesus was the Messiah or Saviour, but they divided along the line of the old Mosaic ritual, which separated the Jew from the rest of mankind. The gospel was first and for many years offered to the Jews only. The result was churches into which none but Jews entered. This was the case with the great mother-church at Jerusalem (Acts 21 : 20).

The same must have been true throughout Judea (1 Thess. 2 : 14). There is evidence, too, that away in Asia Minor and in other parts of the Roman empire there were churches among whose membership only Jews or proselytes were to be found. These Jewish churches had not abandoned Moses, though they had accepted Christ. They were all "zealous of the law." But while they observed its behests they did not rely on it for salvation; Christ was their trust and hope.

1. This state of things gives the historic setting of what might be called the first group of New Testament epistles,—James, Hebrews, 1 Peter, 2 Peter, Jude. They were addressed to these Jewish bodies of believers. Hence we find that they are elementary, that they resemble not a little the language and the thought of the Old Testament prophets, and that they are entirely free from those questions which Paul considered in his writings.

It is not meant that this group is chronologically first, though this may be true of the Epistle of James. It is possible that it was the first book of the New Testament to be written. But the actual time of the composition of a book is not so material as the relative time. The relative time of each book in the group, or, what is the same thing, its place relative to the development of church life and growth, must be observed. These Jewish churches unfolded slowly " in the grace and knowledge of our Lord and Saviour Jesus Christ" (2 Pet. 3 : 18). They lacked the stimulating atmosphere of freedom, which soon put the Gentile churches far in the van.

Hence this first group of Epistles is elementary, and so first, whatever may be the actual date. James's theme is faith. The believing Jews are still connected with the synagogue (James 2 : 2, Rev. Ver.), and works are declared to be the very spirit of the faith which they professed (James 2 : 26). In the Epistle to the Hebrews there is an advance. Faith in Jesus has led into trouble, and there is sore temptation to abandon him and rely on the Jewish ritual alone, which they had never ceased to observe. They are shown, however, that that ritual points to Jesus, and that he is the completion of it. He has brought about its finality.

Peter teaches the believing Jews, first, that they are a new nation (1 Pet. 2 : 9, 10; see also Matt. 21 : 43) in Christ; and secondly, in his old age (2 Pet. 1 : 15), when they have now reached a degree of maturity, he still calls on them to advance, and to await the consummation of what is not "cunningly devised fables."

Jude looks at the danger to faith ensuing from lax morals in the church, and his Epistle is a paraphrase of Matthew 24 : 11-13. These five are not strictly church epistles, not being so directed, and the word "church" occurs in them but three times.

What may be noted in all the New Testament epistles, an earnest trust in Christ's speedy coming, is emphatically prominent in this Jewish-Christian group. Whether right or wrong, these believers looked for the Lord's return in their day;

at least, they were exhorted to be ready for it. Exhortation and exposition revolve largely on this attitude of these primitive churches. It is in view of this that James urges patience (James 1 and 5 : 7, 8). In Hebrews it is this Jesus, whom they are thinking of abandoning, that is to be head of the new state of things to come (Heb. 2 : 5-15); the elders lived in the faith of things to come, suffering all their days without realizing the clear promises made them (Heb. 11); but for the Hebrews the consummation is "approaching" (Heb. 10 : 25, 37), when they are to receive a "kingdom" (Heb. 12 : 27, 28).

Peter assures his readers that the salvation for which they are looking is "ready" to be "revealed in the last time" (1 Pet. 1 : 5), exhorts them to "hope" for it (1 Pet. 1 : 13), and reminds them that he made known to them "the power and coming of our Lord Jesus Christ" by what he personally saw in the "holy mount" (2 Pet. 1 : 16-18). The delay or "long-suffering" of the Lord is to be accounted as "salvation" (2 Pet. 3 : 15). In Jude, in view of the thickening gloom about them (2 Tim. 3 : 1-9) they are to keep themselves in the love of God (Matt. 24 : 12) by looking for the "mercy" which leads to eternal life (Jude, verses 14, 15, and 21). It was Peter, the apostle of the circumcision, who, soon after Pentecost, put the Jews into this attitude of expectation (Acts 3 : 19-21),—an attitude that must not be overlooked in reading these Epistles. The Book of Acts is our key here.

2. The second group of Epistles is the Pauline. In our King James Version, this group of thirteen stands together, beginning with the Epistle to the Romans and closing with the Epistle to Philemon. This group can be considered in three divisions: (1) the missionary epistles, written in this chronological order: 1 Thessalonians, 2

Thessalonians, Galatians, 1 Corinthians, 2 Corinthians, Romans. These were sent forth between the years 52 and 58 of our era, while Paul was spreading the gospel from Antioch in Syria to Corinth in Achaia; (2) the consummation epistles, in which the church has reached its full development,— Colossians, Philippians, Ephesians. These were written from Rome during the years 62 and 63; (3) the individual epistles, Philemon (Rome, 62), 1 Timothy, Titus, 2 Timothy. The date of the last three is not certain.

The Book of Acts again gives us the setting of these Epistles, especially those of the first division. The fifteenth chapter shows the serious division of opinion between the Jewish and the Gentile sections of the church. The Jews did not deny the gospel to the Gentiles, but insisted "that it was needful to circumcise them, and to command them to keep the law of Moses"

(Acts 15 : 5). This proposition had numerous and powerful advocates for years. Paul denied it, and established churches whose foundation was simple faith in Christ. His opponents followed him, and attempted in many places to undo his work. This question, therefore, occupies a large place in the six earlier Epistles, and some place in all, and is the key to much that is written. If Paul argues vehemently for his apostleship, as he does with the Galatians (Gal. 1 and 2), and the Corinthians (1 Cor. 9), to both of whom he mentions Peter, never in commendation, and once to the serious discredit of the chief of the apostles, it is because Paul's Jewish enemies denied his office, and claimed exclusive authority for the apostle to the circumcision. The other means used to destroy Paul's work was to dispute or neutralize his teaching of justification by faith (see Galatians and Romans).

These six Epistles show a clear development from first to last. In Thessalonica we have a company of simple-hearted, loving believers, who have "turned to God from idols," and are waiting for his Son from heaven. The latter is the only marked doctrine in the two epistles to the Thessalonians. They misunderstood it, or went astray on it, and in the second epistle Paul sets them right. The Jews at this stage do not yet seek to pervert; they persecute, and Paul speaks with great severity of them (1 Thess. 2 : 15, 16), and consoles the church in the afflictions put upon it by the Jews.

The Epistle to the Galatians shows an advance, the freedom from the law in Christ Jesus, and exhorts to stedfastness in this freedom, and not to be entangled again in the yoke of bondage (the law). Among the Galatians both Paul and his doctrine had been assailed by the Jews.

At Corinth a false Judaism had succeeded in creating divisions in the church, one following Peter and discrediting Paul. The freedom in Christ Jesus which the Galatians were about to abandon, was perverted in Corinth to license. Even the scruples of the believing Jews were treated with contempt (1 Cor. 8). Before our present first epistle was written, Paul had already communicated with the Corinthians by writing from Ephesus (1 Cor. 5 : 9-13), and probably had made them a short visit from the same city (2 Cor. 2 : 1 ; 13 : 1, 2).

If among the Thessalonians we have a body "turned to God," and among the Galatians a body possessing freedom in Christ Jesus, in Corinth we have a body organized by the Holy Spirit (1 Cor. 12) for all loving and pure works. In Rome we find a body in which the doctrine of grace is finally formulated against the unbelieving Jew, and the relation of Jew and

Gentile exhaustively considered (Rom. 9 to 11). As to doctrine, the Epistle to the Romans is the fundamental epistle, and, so far, stands correctly at the head; but chronologically, and so far as church development is concerned, it is the latest of these missionary epistles.

Those which we have called the consummation epistles,—Colossians, Philippians, Ephesians,—written after the last apostolic church was formed, and when Paul was now a prisoner in Rome, are the flower of this group, and so the most difficult to understand. The first is the philosophic epistle, in which the church is shown to be perfect in Christ as the creator of all things, and so before all things (Col. 1 : 14-19), whether law or angels. Judaism in this epistle has become philosophic in uniting with heathen culture.

Among the Philippians we have a church living like Christ; he is set forth as the comprehensive pattern (Phil. 2), and Paul himself is struggling to be like him (chap. 3), accounting his former righteousness by the law "but dung."

In the church at Ephesus, the last one formed by Paul, and with which he remained three years, we have the climax and completion of the church. It is the wonder of the angels (Eph. 3 : 10), and Paul records two earnest prayers in the epistle to this church (Eph. 1 : 15-23; 3 : 14-21), that the saints themselves may have the enlightenment and spiritual "might" to comprehend the glory of the church. Judaism cannot be mentioned in this Epistle.

Paul wrote four individual epistles. Slavery existed everywhere. The Epistle to Philemon shows with gentle courtesy how a Christian master should receive back a runaway slave, converted to Christ by Paul while a prisoner in Rome. The other three epistles are directions to Timothy and Titus about their behavior as ministers of the church (1 Tim. 3 : 15, 16); how careful they should be in providing for the ministry of the church (1 Tim. 3 : 1-13; Tit. 1 : 5-9), and the preservation of its deposit of truth (2 Tim. 2). The Scriptures are warmly commended to them as a guide. Unworthy leaders are plainly described (1 Tim. 6 : 3-5; 2 Tim. 4 : 3, 4; Tit. 1 : 10-16), and the teachers of the law are characterized as "understanding neither what they say, nor whereof they affirm" (1 Tim. 1 : 7).

3. The third or latest group of New Testament epistles is the three by John. The second warns against false doctrine, and denies entertainment to those who hold it; the third commends Christian hospitality. These two are individual epistles. The First Epistle of John, which was, most likely, the last of the church

epistles in the New Testament to be written, is at once the simplest and the most profound,—simple in expression, profound in its ideas. It was published at Ephesus a full quarter of a century after the last of Paul's letters was written. It is profoundly spiritual, and shows the church in full fellowship with God, walking in the light of his being and reflecting his love. The Jewish enemies that confronted the church in Paul's day have disappeared. New ones have sprung up within the church itself (Acts 20 : 30; 1 John 2 : 18, 19),—the antichrists have come, and the battle is now about the person of the Redeemer. The defense is found not in apostolic authority, not in the covenants, not in the Bible, but in the certain spiritual apprehension and loving walk of those who know God. The word "know" occurs thirty-nine times in the Epistle. It closes with a chorus, "we know," repeated six times.

Ignorance and unbelief are the essence of idolatry. As the first church epistle, chronologically, was written to those who "*turned* to God from idols" (1 Thess. 1 : 9), so this latest one ends, "Little children, *keep* yourselves from idols."

Crozer Theological Seminary.

THE BIBLE AS A GUIDE IN SOCIAL STUDIES

THE BIBLE AS A GUIDE IN SOCIAL STUDIES

BY PRESIDENT ROBERT ELLIS THOMPSON, S.T.D.

The Bible is not, as some have assumed, a declaration merely of God's purpose to save individual men out of this world into a better one. It discloses his purpose to save society no less than individuals. Our Lord preached the advent of a kingdom of God, a kingdom of heaven, meaning manifestly a new and truer order of human social life than the earth as yet possessed. His teaching is largely occupied with the relations of men inside this society, with the laws of truth, openness, mutual confidence, and generosity, which are to control its conduct.

This side of the Bible's teaching appeals

with especial force to our own generation, in that we are drawn so much to the study of social problems. Professor Drummond says that in his labors among the students of the University of Edinburg he found them especially open to this aspect of the truth. They were roused by the promise of a social life better and more human than they had known, where they would have remained comparatively indifferent to a gospel offered to them as individuals. In this latter they were wrong, but not wrong in being alive to the gospel as a social program.

But the sociology of the Bible does not begin with the Gospels. The whole book, from Genesis to Revelation, abounds in interest of this kind. Sir Henry Sumner Maine, in his "Ancient Law," refers to the Book of Genesis as the only complete and trustworthy account we have of the process by which the family was expanded into a tribe, a group of tribes, a nation. What the sociologists gather by inference from other documents, notably from the Brehon Laws of Ireland, is here described explicitly.

The history of the Jewish state occupies the greater part of the Old Testament, and fills a large place in the New. It is not possible to grasp the full significance of the Bible story unless we see in it the record of a nation under divine training and discipline. Neither will it do to put this story apart from the story of other nations as a thing special, exceptional, and supernatural. The supernatural enters into the history of every people. The Hebrew historians differ from the ordinary writers of history in having the insight to see and the courage to declare God's dealing with their people in orderly or unexpected ways. The Hebrew history is the best key to God's dealing with nations in all ages.

And the best comment on the Hebrew story often is found in the experiences of peoples of a later date.

Sir Edward Strachey has shown this admirably in his work on the prophecies of Isaiah, originally published under the title, "Hebrew Politics in the Times of Sargon and Sennacherib." He draws freely upon Niebuhr and other students of the politics of modern Europe for his materials. The prophets, indeed, were sociologists by profession, and public teachers of their people with regard to present duties and national problems. They brought to their people the message which the really great reformers of all ages have proclaimed. They declared the intimate relation of society to God, who stands with the plumb-line in his hand among the peoples, demanding of men the absolute uprightness of which that is the symbol. With Plato, Savonarola, Cromwell, Mazzini,

Lincoln, they called their people to love righteousness, and to array themselves on God's side, instead of offering him futile bribes to take their side.

The family and the nation are limited and local societies. But the human instinct calls for a universal society, which shall exist to gather all men into one brotherhood. That is given in the church which Jesus founded, sending forth the Twelve to gather all nations into its membership. In the church is the gathering under one Head (ἀνακεφαλαιῶσθαι) of whatever is in the heavens and whatever is upon the earth (Eph. 1 : 10). In the establishment of the church the last great step is taken in the sociological development of mankind, whatever lesser steps remained to be taken. To the institute of the affections, which is the family, and the institute of rights, which is the state, was added the institute of humanity, which is the church.

The Acts of the Apostles, therefore, possesses for the sociologist exactly the interest which Sir Henry Sumner Maine ascribes to the Book of Genesis. Here also we have a trustworthy and intelligible account of the origination of a new form of society, and one as necessary and as natural as the state itself. Here we have the first and formative stages of a great development, which has gone forward ever since. And as we go back to the Ten Words at Sinai to learn what were the rights which the state exists to realize, and what are its essential relations to its Creator, so we go to the teachings of the Gospels and the Acts to learn what are the laws of this new form of social life. And as the later Jewish history presents a running commentary upon the Sinaitic law, so the Epistles and the Revelation supply the authentic comment on the law of the church's life in all ages.

The Apocalypse, especially, is a sociological book. It opens with the social life and social trials and victories of seven of the early churches. It passes to a glimpse of the society of heaven in its holy joy and awful subordinations. It returns to our planet to depict the judgments about to fall upon two perverted and ungodly forms of society,—the Jewish nation and the Roman empire. It closes with a vision, not of heaven, but of the holy society about to be established upon earth,—the New Jerusalem coming down out of heaven to this earth. The book deals everywhere with the social fellowships of mankind, not with the well-being or ill-being of individuals within them.

To study the Bible in its entirety, one must be more or less of a sociologist. Not that sociology is to supersede everything else, and especially not that the individual, with his rights and responsibilities, his spiritual needs and powers, is to be left out of sight. He is there, present on every page, and yet rarely filling the whole page, often occupying but a small part of it. For the Bible is broad as life, having, indeed, the same author.

Philadelphia, Pa.

UNATTAINED IDEAL OF BIBLE STUDY

UNATTAINED IDEAL OF BIBLE STUDY

BY BISHOP JOHN H. VINCENT, D.D, LL.D.

There is to be no early reaction from the scientific interest and activities of these times. At the close of this century we are climbing the heights; the beginning of the next century will lift us higher still in our attainments and requirements, and I have good faith also in all spiritual accessions and possessions.

Science will no longer be the pursuit of the few, confined in laboratories, exploring and scrutinizing nature for mere intellectual results. It is abroad now in the fields and on the streets; and our boys are after it to know its secrets, and to have a hand in the work it is doing, and has yet to do.

Boys who meant never to study much, but to be clerks, and merchants, and speculators, have been struck by lightning from the laboratories of Edison and others, and they are in colleges, or in scientific schools, getting ready intelligently to handle wires, batteries, and engines, and to make some discoveries of their own.

The young men of parts and tact are rushing into these fields with such rapidity that some of us are wondering what we shall do for ministers to attract and hold them, and their kind, and the age they represent; for the next century is to be an era of science and of applied science.

This scientific era is not, I believe, to be a materialistic era. The invisible forces are being felt. The analogies between energies of nature and of a spiritual realm multiply, and the transitions are so gradual, from the most ethereal forms of matter and the forces which control them to the realm we call spiritual, that faith in the latter is greatly promoted by discoveries in the former. This age of electricity is an age of opening eyes and upreaching souls. We are leaving the arid plains of materialism. The atmosphere in the scientific world grows warmer, and the Nazarene holds a higher place than ever. Mere ecclesiasticism more and more excites the contempt of the world. Souls of men are feeling after the true God, whose presence is neither on altars, within cathedrals, nor on " this mountain," nor at " Jerusalem."

Can the church meet this age and hold its own? Not by science, although the church should prize and promote every branch of true science. Not by governments, although the church, through her individual members, should have a share in the making of good government. But by her distinctive mission—the opening and applying of the truth, adapting it to the age, emphasizing the essentials on the spiritual and moral side, expecting that God will be with us and in us, and that his love shall be the law of our lives. The coming age is one of intellectual activity, of independence, of scientific advancement.

The true study of the Bible is still an unattained mission of the church. We do study it, but in texts and for texts. We quote it in disconnected fragments, we misquote through lack of accuracy in committing, we mislearn misquoted texts, we quote old human saws of general literature as Scripture sayings, we put old constructions on old passages, and assume that our views, because they are old, must be true.

But as for the study of the Bible as literature—what do we know about that process? We assume that the valuable parts of the Bible are the flowerets that bloom in sweet promises, and proverbs that shoot up like sturdy plants among the rocks. We pluck the flowers, and study the plants, and pass by the rocks.

It is the province of the schools of theology to study the order of the development and the details of the Book. We do not like—the most of us—philological, archæological, geographical study. We care very little, in truth, for historical studies; and we wonder that, if God did give the Bible to the world, he should have packed into it so much that is formal, ancient, dry, chronological, and unprofitable.

We half believe with a certain class of skeptics, who pronounce these old books effete, useless, mythical, and valuable only as curiosities in a geological museum, for the dry and odd folks who take interest in fossils, and are out of sympathy with this living and busy age.

The ministry of the church ministers to this idea by limiting its work to preaching, praying, and visiting; to discussing current topics, popular topics, curious topics, and thus drawing crowds on Sunday; to dining out with the well-to-do, or now and then, as a matter of condescension, with the devout and ill-to-do members of the church; to marrying the young, baptizing babes and new believers, and burying the dead, —all the while the church being closed, the furnace frozen, the bells silent, and all the halls and rooms of the great structure vacant by day and silent by night, except on Sunday and on one evening every week, or in those rare seasons of revival which come and go to some churches because they make a great point of that, and to some churches because other churches hold them, and to all churches, at some time during every twenty years, because they cannot very well help themselves.

All this time that the church building is unused, and the church-members looking for revivals, conducting them, or gathering up the results of them, the great multitude of church-members and their children, and of people who really wish they and their children were church-members, are giving themselves up to secularity, to idleness, to society, to frivolity.

And all this time a great book is in the church, a library of great books in one, closed and unused, with the multiplied copies in the homes of the people; a marvelous book, inviting study, systematic, popular, helpful,—a book full of wonder and wisdom.

Our theory of the church is that it is an instructional and spiritual institution, rather than sacerdotal and sacramental. We meet in it for intelligent worship. In order to intelligence there must be instruction.

We will not now discuss the question as between the sacerdotal and the democratic conception of the church, between its aim under the sacramental theory and under the theory personal and instructional, but we do insist that the church is designed to promote intelligent worship, and a life of seven days a week of intelligent, earnest, active service of God and man. The church is a school, believers are disciples, its course of study extends all the year round, and all the round years into eternity. The text-book is the Bible, the Word of God, on the one hand, and this vast universe of matter and mind, the work of God, on the other.

The pulpit, enshrined in a service of worship, should be the medium of instruction in the reading of the Scripture, for which our common Christianity should provide a prescribed course of reading-lessons for every Sabbath morning and evening. The very singing of hymns by the people should minister to the intelligence of the people. The words of prayer should lift by the thought in them, as well as by their fervor; the sermons should be biblical, full of the simple Word of God, dealing in doctrine, in parables, in ethics, in history, in biography. No topics are more attractive, more suggestive, more replete with moral and religious teachings, more pictorial and vivid, more likely to remain with young people, than the biographical characters which form the chain of Bible history, for these teach of the old historic nations, Egypt, Arabia, Babylon, Syria, Western Asia, Macedonia, Greece, and Rome, and all the wealth of modern geographical study and inspiration is ready for the minister's use, for the delight and education of the young. The age of pulpit rant and cant, of theological vagueness, of platitudes, exaggerations, and pedantry, has passed. The pew is on the alert, and ready to give thoughtful attention to the efforts of a thoughtful pulpit.

The home should be a school of the Bible, a department of the church. We must put forth effort to awaken the American church to the great fact of parental responsibility. The English Bible must be placed and opened, applied, expounded, illustrated, in the American home. A big book in a place of power. At family prayer every day, the Book; on Sabbath days, the Book.

Home must teach God's word. To this great necessity the pulpit must awaken, tracts must be circulated, pastoral appeals must be made; for the English Bible, with all the possibilities of spiritual life that are in it, is a dead thing if it be left unopened and unstudied. Table talk at home, Sunday-schools, Bible memorizing, the telling over and over to the little ones of the old stories of the old book, co-operation with the Sunday-school in the preparation of lessons,—all these things are indispensable.

They are little things, but so are the coral-builders and their daily labors; they are little things, but so are flakes of snow that arrest limited-express trains, or drops of water that make the mighty sea.

I saw a picture, once, of an old Bible, lids loosened, and leaves uneven; but the whole had been carefully placed on a marble table, and on top of the venerable book a pair of spectacles were folded. The fingers that turned these pages are still now, the eyes that looked through these glasses into the mysteries of the Word are closed, but the spirit that was illumined by these eternal verities sees the King in his beauty.

Oh the suggestions of the Book in the home!

Buffalo, N. Y.

www.ingramcontent.com/pod-product-compliance
Lightning Source LLC
Chambersburg PA
CBHW031349230426
43670CB00006B/479